Teilhard
and the Future of Humanity

Teilhard and the Future of Humanity

Edited by

Thierry Meynard, S.J.

FORDHAM UNIVERSITY PRESS

New York 2006

Library of Congress Cataloging-in-Publication Data

Teilhard and the future of humanity / edited by
Thierry Meynard.—1st ed.
p. cm.
Includes bibliographical references and index.
ISBN-13: 978-0-8232-2690-0
ISBN-10: 0-8232-2690-5
1. Teilhard de Chardin,
Pierre. 2. Humanity. 3. Civilization—Forecasting.
I. Meynard, Thierry.
B2430.T374T36   2006
194—dc22
2006021329

Printed in the United States of America
08 07 06   5 4 3 2 1
First edition.

CONTENTS

Preface
THIERRY MEYNARD, S.J.   vii

TEILHARD AND HUMAN SPIRIT

1. Feeding the Zest for Life:
    Spiritual Energy Resources for the Future of
    Humanity
    URSULA KING   3

2. God and the Human Future
    THOMAS M. KING, S.J.   20

3. The Personalization of the Universe;
    or, The Era of the Person
    HENRI MADELIN, S.J.   29

TEILHARD AND ECOLOGY

4. Zest for Life: Teilhard's Cosmological Vision
    MARY EVELYN TUCKER   43

5. Teilhard's Vision and the Earth Charter
    STEVEN C. ROCKEFELLER   56

TEILHARD AND ECONOMIC GLOBALIZATION

6. Teilhard, Globalization, and the Future of Humanity
    MICHEL CAMDESSUS   71

7. Teilhard and Globalization
    JEAN BOISSONNAT   89

v

TEILHARD AND SCIENCE

8.   The Emergence of Consciousness in Biological
     Evolution and Quantum Reality
         LOTHAR SCHÄFER   109

9.   The Role of Science in Contemporary China
     and according to Teilhard
         THIERRY MEYNARD, S.J.   135

     Notes   157

     Bibliography   171

     Contributors   179

     Index   183

Fifty years after the death of the French Jesuit and scientist Teilhard de Chardin, what can be said today about his thought? At first glance, Teilhard's optimism about the future of humanity does not match the reality and the trends of our present world. Teilhard, able to transcend political boundaries, envisioned a growing awareness of the fundamental unity of the human family. Yet, at present, it seems that our world has never been so divided, so torn apart by religious fundamentalisms. The economic and social gap between Africa and the rest of the world is widening, not shrinking. Teilhard stressed the fundamental continuity between the material and the human worlds, but the depletion of natural resources and the damage done to the environment have alienated humankind further from nature. Teilhard called for a renewal of modern man and woman, whose spiritual resources would build the future, but we have never felt so powerless in the face of the dominating forces of materialism and consumerism. It is quite tempting, then, to dismiss the work of Teilhard as idealism or wishful thinking—not only unpractical but perhaps even dangerous.

But Teilhard would call us to a deeper wisdom. While it is inevitable that we observe what is disappearing and dying out, the irreversible destruction of the past, and violent conflicts, such observations may simply touch on the mere surface. Teilhard was more interested in what is being built among the shambles of the present, and what is emerging from the incoherence of contemporary events. This optimism about the evolution of humankind was not purely an act of personal faith, but was founded also on those facts of science that he was discerning in the natural and human worlds. Nonetheless, Teilhard was still a realist and contemplated also the possibilities of a failed humanity, should the forces of egoism and fear prevail.

Throughout 2005, people across the world commemorated the fiftieth anniversary of the death of Pierre Teilhard de Chardin. In April, the French and the American Teilhard Associations hosted the climax of these events, bringing some 2000 people from five continents to New York, where Teilhard died on April 10th, 1955.

The papers collected here were given at Fordham University on April 7th (Lothar Schäfer, Ursula King, Jean Boissonnat, Thomas King, Henri Madelin), at Iona College, New Rochelle, New York, on the same day (Mary-Evelyn Tucker), at the Headquarters of the United Nations, also on the same day (Michel Camdessus), and in the same venue, on April 8 (Steven C. Rockefeller). They represent the attempts of scholars from different fields to express Teilhard's thought in respect to the future of humanity.

These papers have been grouped into four topics: Human Spirit, Ecology, Economic Globalization, and Science, illustrating the diversity of Teilhard's relevance for today. The first set of papers deals with Teilhard's vision in regard to the development of the human spirit, from the inside layers of individual self-awareness to that of others, and to the world. Ursula King, in "Feeding the Zest for Life: Spiritual Energy Resources for the Future of Humanity," links Teilhard's vision with the future as we see it emerging in today's world. In Thomas King's "God and the Human Future," we see how deeply Teilhard was shaped by the enthusiasms of the human spirit, which was in search for scientific truth, and which lead some to sacrifice themselves for their nation. King describes how these ideals led Teilhard to discover a Someone who animates from within. This theme of a Personal God is further developed in "The Personalization of the Universe; or the Era of the Person." Here, Henri Madelin describes how, for Teilhard, the self grows and acquires new layers of meaning in contact with a globalized world, experienced, in Teilhard's term, as a thinking envelope. This concept of a growing humanity is expressed also in Teilhard's own affectivity. He sought not only to understand life, but to love and cherish it, as expressed so powerfully in his letters and poetic prayers. While he remained faithful to his vow of chastity, friendships with women strongly influenced Teilhard's life. He understood the role of the feminine in the universe, and his understanding of the feminine was situated at the junction between cosmic and human senses of that term. He rejected worn-out interpretations of marriage and religious perfection, the former being defined too narrowly as merely the social precondition for reproduction, and the latter as the theological necessity for a kind of separatism. With a rich understanding of the specific capacities of men and women, Teilhard believed chastity could lead to harmony between the genders and a new type of communion.

The second set of papers addresses the question of humanity in its relation to the Earth. In "Zest for Life: Teilhard's Cosmological Vision," Mary-Evelyn Tucker locates six dimensions of Teilhard's cosmology relevant to today's concerns. She describes a vital movement within us, which connects us with the creativity of the cosmos. Steven Rockefeller, in "Teilhard's Vision and the Earth Charter," offers an overview of the writing and content of the Earth Charter (2000), as a declaration of fundamental principles for building a just, sustainable, and peaceful global community. He shows how those principles echo Teilhard's ideas.

Teilhard was one of the first to theorize about a phenomenon he called "planetization," later called globalization in the field of international economy. In "Pierre Teilhard de Chardin, Globalization, and the Future of Humanity," Michel Camdessus describes the economic and political challenges faced by the world, and, drawing from Teilhard, advocates a humanized globalization. Jean Boissonnat, as an economist, offers, in "Teilhard and Globalization," his own reading of the last work of Teilhard, *The Christic*.

Boissonnat holds that Christianity has a powerful contribution to offer, since it can make globalization meaningful and humane.

Finally, in the last section, the question of Teilhard's contested understanding of science is addressed. In "The Emergence of Consciousness in Biological Evolution and Quantum Reality," Lothar Schäfer describes the latest discoveries in the structure of matter and molecules, which suggest a certain degree of consciousness already present at the level of elementary particles and human cells. Teilhard's ideas about evolution corroborate those new findings. While the past century has seen mainstream science concentrate on the "outside of things," Teilhard caused science to change direction by paying equal attention to what he called the "within of things." For Teilhard, as for many scientists today, it is a scientific fact that the universe is infused with consciousness. My own paper, "The Role of Science, in Contemporary China and according to Teilhard," attempts to situate Teilhard's thinking in the context of the debate on science in contemporary China. While Teilhard himself was not directly involved in this debate, he had worked with some important players, mostly Chinese colleagues leaning toward scientism. However, at the same time, some Chinese intellectuals were trying, in a way much as Teilhard was, to understand the relation between matter and consciousness.

One can only be impressed by how Teilhard's concern for the future of humanity continues to attract people who seldom meet professionally—the scientists, the economists, the environmentalists, and the theologians. This fact in itself reflects the core of Teilhard's life and thinking, in which so many diverse interests converged toward the Omega, Christ, the unique mystery in which everything is accomplished. The Jesuit scientist succeeded in unfolding an ancient message for our modern world. Silenced by the Church, he had few friends when he died and was unknown to most people. Since his death in 1955, his ideas have propagated throughout the world, animating the minds and hearts of many.

As Teilhard himself said: "Sooner or later there will be a chain-reaction. This is one more proof that Truth has to appear only once, in one single mind, for it to be impossible for anything ever to prevent it from spreading universally and setting everything ablaze" ("Le Christique," in *Le Coeur de la Matiére* vol. 13 of *Oeuvres*, 117).

I would like to thank Fordham University Press for publishing this volume, which follows a previous study written by Robert J. O'Connell, S.J., *Teilhard's Vision of the Past*, 1982. Professor Daniel O'Brien of Fordham University has contributed many suggestions to improve this present volume. Also, a special thanks to the translators and to Professor Joseph Koterski, S.J., for all the encouragement and support which has made this publication possible. Last, I would like to warmly thank Fordham University Press, and especially Robert Oppedisano, its director, and Nicholas Frankovich, its managing editor, for the special care they have given to the publication of this volume.

Thierry Meynard, S.J.

TEILHARD
AND THE FUTURE OF HUMANITY

.

Teilhard and Human Spirit

Feeding the Zest for Life: Spiritual Energy Resources for the Future of Humanity

Ursula King

Reflections on the future of humankind, and its further social, cultural and spiritual development, feature prominently in the work of Pierre Teilhard de Chardin. His thoughts on these matters can be a splendid resource for our contemporary efforts to move forward in building a more interdependent network of mutual responsibility and care within the global community. He expressed with clarity and forcefulness that we are *one* humanity, with *one* origin, and *one* destiny. We have not yet reached maturity in terms of our possibilities; our immense problems somehow resemble the turmoils of youth. Teilhard argued that all of humankind should bear a profound sense of responsibility for the shape of its own future, and that this future must be developed in close interrelation with all forms of life, and with the whole of nature in its global and planetary dimensions. Central to his thinking about creating in the future a more integrated form of oneness for humanity are several key ideas: the *zest for life* in advancing the growth of humanity to achieve a better life for all; the *noosphere* as an expanding sphere of human thought and invention, of will and

4 Ursula King

work, of love and action; the need for material and spiritual *energy resources* in assuring the future of humanity; and the contribution of world faiths in providing *spiritual energy resources* for feeding the zest for life. I shall deal with each briefly as they are mutually embedded and interdependent on each other.

1. The Future of Humanity and the Zest for Life

Teilhard de Chardin wrote about the future of humanity in a collection of essays called *The Future of Man*. These essays are preceded by the motto: "The whole future of the Earth, as of religion, seems to me to depend on the awakening of our faith in the future."[1] He combined such *faith in the future* with what he called *faith in man* (that is, in the potential and further development of human beings), with *faith in peace*, and with *faith in the greater unity and global collaboration among the peoples of the earth*.

Teilhard began to reflect on these matters after the First World War; he subsequently developed and further clarified them during the 1920s, 1930s and especially the 1940s, when he completed his magnum opus, the book *The Human Phenomenon*,[2] written during his stay in China. Teilhard's concern for the future of human beings, and all of life, was expressed with a new urgency after the Second World War, when he became increasingly aware of the radical transformations occurring within the human community on planet earth. It was in post-war Paris that he also got involved with a pioneering group, *Le Congrès Universel des Croyants*. Set up by Sir Francis Younghusband in London in 1936, it was interreligious in nature, and founded as a French branch of the British *World Congress of Faiths*. Teilhard's association with this group remains largely unknown, but he refers to it in his correspondence, and he wrote five essays between 1947 and 1950 specifically addressed to them.[3] In 1947 he was invited to provide the inaugural address, represented by his essay "Faith in Man"[4] for Le Congrès Universel des Croyants. Here, as elsewhere, he expresses his faith in the further intellectual, moral and spiritual development of human beings around the globe. He writes: "A profound common aspiration arising out of the very shape of the modern world—is not this specifically what is most to be desired, what we most need to offset the growing forces of dissolution and dispersal at work among us?"[5]

How equally true this is today! We are experiencing inequality and injustice, numerous wars, violence, disaster, and immense human suffering in so many parts of the globe. Yet the hope and longing of so many millions, and the need for greater human unity and integration, for mutual help and encouragement, for the sharing of material and spiritual resources—and that includes the sharing of ideas and visions—are greater than ever. More than fifty years ago Teilhard sensed this great contradiction between our deepest longings for the genuinely new possibilities for humankind and the insufficiency of our efforts: the lack of will and action, the shortcoming of our thinking and practical initiatives to make the world a better place. The same year, 1947, that he wrote his address on "Faith in Man" (a year before the United Nations' Universal Declaration of Human Rights) Teilhard also drafted a three page statement on "Some Reflections on the Rights of Man,"[6] published by UNESCO in 1949, wherein he refers to a "new Charter of Humanity" and argues for the mutual interdependence of the development of the individual person and that of the larger human group. Teilhard speaks of "the well-ordered integration" of the individual "with the unified group in which Mankind must eventually culminate, both organically and spiritually" and of the "two processes of collectivization and personalization" as interdependent.[7] However, he was well aware that this is not an automatic process in which a positive outcome is guaranteed, but, on the contrary, it presents itself as a huge task for the human community, an ideal to aim and work for, and one beset by immense problems.

Where does one find the ethical criteria for making the right choices in shaping the future of humanity? How does one find the necessary energy resources for feeding the zest for life and human action? He addressed these questions in his 1950 lecture on "The Zest for Living," given to another meeting of the Congrès Universel des Croyants.[8] We cannot live without a zest for life, we cannot advance the world without it. We need to love life, live it to the full, and contribute to its growth. In a metaphorical sense he sees the zest for life as "nothing less than the *energy of universal evolution*," but, at the human level, the feeding and development of this energy "is to some degree *our responsibility*."[9]

How can this be done? And where do we find the necessary resources for this "feeding and development" of the zest for life in the global community today, when we are faced with so many different groups and nations, with opposing political interests and powers, clashing beliefs and mutually exclusive identities? Building a common future for humanity presents us with a tremendous task, greater than any ever met before in the history of humankind. To refer to this task as "building" may be too external and positivistic a description. Given the biological, organic texture of life, as well as the current interest in the new field of emergence in science, and the research into as yet undiscovered "information-gathering" processes in nature, it may be more appropriate to speak about "growing" rather than "building the future." The verb *growing* better expresses the emergent, dynamic nature of creating and working for the future of humanity—a process which is not entirely within human control, but contains elements of novelty, chance and uncertainty within it. I also prefer the reference to "growing" because of Howard Thurman's expression of looking to "the growing edge,"[10] rather than the customary, more instrumental "cutting edge," in moving life and research forward. This is a more organic, potentially richer way of thinking that relates more creatively to our contemporary ecological sensibilities. Teilhard de Chardin spoke of a new threshold in the development of human consciousness and organization. Instead of being mostly concerned with living longer, with mere survival, human beings should attempt to create a higher form of life, a more unified humanity. As he wrote in *The Human Phenomenon*:

> Like children come of age and workers who have grown "conscious," we are in the midst of discovering that something is developing in the world by means of us—perhaps at our own expense. And even more serious, we are now aware that in the great game we are engaged in, not only are we the players, but the cards and the stakes as well. If we get up from the table, nothing will go on. And there is nothing, either, to force us to stay seated. Is the game worth it? . . .
>
> . . . The danger is that the elements of the world may refuse to serve the world through the very fact that they think; or, even more precisely, that the world may refuse itself in becoming aware of itself through reflection. What is forming and swelling beneath our modern uneasiness is nothing less than an organic crisis in evolution.[11]

Where to gather the necessary energy resources to advance human life and its further evolution?

2. *Biosphere, Noosphere, and the Sense of the Earth*

The above quotation, from *The Human Phenomenon*, implicitly expresses that the organic evolution of life engages in the reflective effort of thinking. In other words, it implies that biological, social and cultural evolution are all closely interrelated. We hear a great deal about the *biosphere* these days, especially in environmental and ecological debates, but few people will know that Teilhard de Chardin was an early promoter of the idea of the biosphere, a term first coined in 1875 by the Austrian scientist Eduard Suess, who later wrote a large study called *The Face of the Earth*.[12] In 1921 Teilhard used this same title for an essay published in the Jesuit journal *Études*, wherein he wrote:

Suess . . . saw the biosphere stretching like a veritable stratum of animated matter, the stratum of living beings and humanity. The great educational value of geology consists in the fact that by disclosing to us an earth which is truly *one*, an earth which is in fact but a single body since it has a face, it recalls to us the possibilities of establishing higher and higher degrees of organic unity in the zone of thought which envelops the world. In truth it is impossible to keep one's gaze constantly fixed on the vast horizons opened out to us by science without feeling the stirrings of an obscure desire to see people drawn closer and closer together by an ever-increasing knowledge and sympathy until finally, in obedience to some divine attraction, there remains but one heart and one soul on the face of the earth.[13]

There is an implication here of the new concept of the *noosphere*, which Teilhard created in the mid-twenties in collaboration with his philosopher friend Edouard Le Roy, who was the first to use it in his writings. Soon it was also taken up by several scientists, although it never became as popular as the term *biosphere*. The origin of the idea of the noosphere, as the sphere of the human mind within the biosphere, stems from Teilhard's consciousness of the immensity of the earth and its peoples, their common origin and destiny, and their place in nature. It is rooted in his geological and biological studies, in his extensive travels in North Africa and Asia (especially in China), but also in his life in the trenches of the First World War when, during his night watches, the whole world appeared to him as one great "thing," as if perceived from the moon. He then described the globe as surrounded by a layer of blueness which for him symbolized the density of thought. Many years later, the image of our bluish-green planet suspended in the blackness of space became known all over the world through the famous photograph taken of the earth from the moon, an image so aptly named "Earth-Rise."

The word *noosphere* is derived from the Greek word *nous* or mind, understood as integrating vision, and it refers specifically to the layer of mind, thought and spirit within the layer of life covering the earth. However, it must not be reduced to a merely intellectualized or spiritualized interpretation, as often happens. The noosphere is deeply rooted in, and embedded within, the organic layers of the biosphere of which it represents a further unfolding and flowering. It is not enough, either, to understand it merely as a sphere of knowledge and invention. It represented for Teilhard a sphere of human thought and will, of love, action and interaction: all of which are closely interwoven and interdependent. When discussing the formation of the noosphere, Teilhard presented it as a "biological interpretation of human history."[14]

The mutual embeddedness and co-evolution of biosphere and noosphere, and the contemporary usage of these concepts by western and Russian scientists, is well documented in *The Biosphere and Noosphere Reader* (1999), edited by the environmental scientists Paul R. Samson and David Pitt.[15] Reflecting on different understandings of the noosphere in relation to contemporary global issues, they write:

> Regardless of which world view is taken, the noosphere represents an essential phase in the history of our planet. In essence, it involves the "coming of age" of a species—in this case, *Homo sapiens*—which, in *reflecting* on itself and its environment, fundamentally alters the evolutionary process and future development on Earth. . . . What matters is that the noosphere is an unprecedented event on Earth and that society appears to be entering a critical period in this phase. In many senses, the Earth has become a single system, an interwoven relationship of global mind and global action.[16]

They refer to the United Nations and some of the NGOs, but also to new guidelines such as the Earth Charter, as "noospheric institutions" and speak of "noospheric structures" which are network-like and participatory rather than oppositional and exclusive, thus stressing the holistic nature of the noosphere concept which includes pluralistic and flexible approaches, together with the notion of balance. Drawing on many Teilhardian ideas, they conclude:

> If the unity of humankind will prove to be a crucial factor in human development, community with nature will be at least equally important. The environmental movement is therefore central to the noosphere, alongside the preservation of cultural heritage. This complementarity of diversity is not a contradiction, since the unity and holism of the noosphere—as with the biosphere—is made up of a mosaic of different, and sometimes conflicting, components. It is not unlike Lovelock's notion of the living planet with its diverse elements, interactions and species that produces an emergent sense of the whole.[17]

One of the strongest expressions of Teilhard's sense of the earth, and of humanity as one, is found in his 1931 essay "The Spirit of Earth,"[18] which he had planned to write for a long time. In 1926 he wrote to a friend that he wanted to provide an "Account of the Earth" in which he did not speak as "a Frenchman, not as a unit in any group, but . . . simply as a 'terrestrian,'" who wanted to express "the confidence, desires and plenitude, also the disappointments, worries and a kind of vertigo of a man who considers the destinies and interests of the earth (humanity) as a whole."[19] He describes this sense of the earth as "the passionate sense of common destiny that draws the thinking fraction of life ever further forward." He writes of "the evolution of a greater consciousness," whereby human thought "introduces a new era in the history of nature" which involves a renewal of life, morality, and spirituality, presenting us with a "cosmic problem of action" and a "crisis of birth."[20] Here, and elsewhere in his work, Teilhard de Chardin expresses deep concern for "building the earth" and for developing "the spirit of one earth"—that is, with seeing the whole world and all peoples within it as one. Beyond the external forces of unification, or globalization as we would say today, brought about by scientific research, economics, finance, political power, media communication or militarization, Teilhard was looking for the "miracle of a common soul,"[21] for a greater convergence and union of the diverse elements of humanity. This cannot be achieved without the powers of love and compassion, and without developing the "Spirit of Earth," nor without what he calls "the arising of God," that is to say, the continuous development of the idea of God on earth, or what some might perceive as the openness to the presence of the spirit.

Teilhard points to human hesitation and resistance "to open our hearts wide to the call of the world within us, to the *sense of the earth*."[22] Yet this sense can reveal to us "the newly freed energies of love, the dormant energies of human unity, the hesitant energies of research."[23] He explains these in both metaphorical and religious terms. Love is described as "the most tremendous and the most mysterious of the cosmic forces." "Huge, ubiquitous and always unsubdued," love is a "wild force," but also "a sacred reserve of energy"—it is "like the blood of spiritual evolution."[24] As to human unity, human beings often experience more of "instinctive repulsion," isolation, and distance from each other than genuine attraction; we cannot truly love millions of strangers but are often profoundly disturbed by the plurality we encounter. The "Spirit of Earth" and the experience of human unity seem at present more of a dream than a reality, yet Teilhard felt that this "sense of the Earth," this feeling for greater human unity, is now "in process of formation." It is "the irresistible pressure which unites people at a given moment in a passion they share."[25] This creates a movement toward human convergence and union through a new form of love practiced through mutual "interlinking" rather than mere personal attraction.[26] It is the active moving forward of the noosphere which, in Teilhard's view, may produce "a superabundance of love" that can overcome human isolation and break down the innumerable partitions that still divide human activity. The active forefront of this growth of the noosphere is "a systematic organization and exploration of our universe" and the pursuit of research at all levels. Far from being "an accessory, an eccentricity or a danger," research is for Teilhard "the highest of human functions" which will "absorb the spirit of war and shine with the light of religions."²⁷ Seen from hindsight, this remark, written in 1931, seems incredibly overoptimistic, undiscerning and naïve, especially when taking into account some of the controversial applications of contemporary scientific research, and the excesses of material production and consumption. It invites strong critique. To be fair, Teilhard also diagnosed the many symptoms of a growing crisis, not only in the psychological, intellectual, and spiritual spheres of modern life, but also in the political and economic domains of contemporary society. He wrote in the same essay:

> From the economic and industrial point of view the crisis is evident. . . . Too much iron, too much wheat, too many automobiles—but also too many books, too many observations; and also too many diplomas, technicians and workmen—and even too many children. The world cannot function without producing living beings, food, ideas. But its production is more and more patently exceeding its powers of absorption and assimilation . . . we must ask what this excess production means. Is the world condemned, as it grows, to automatic death by stifling beneath its own excessive weight?

He answered this question in the negative and interpreted the numerous problems as a "crisis of birth," a process of raising "the edifice of life *to a new stage.*" Using the familiar metaphor of "building," he writes:

> The resources at our disposal today, the powers that we have released, *could not possibly be absorbed* by the narrow system of individual or national units which the architects of the human earth have hitherto used. Our plan was to build a *big house*, larger but similar in design to our good old dwelling places. And now we have been led by the higher logic of progress which is in us, to

collect components that are too big for the use we intended to make of them.

The text then moves on to a powerful, visionary statement that is often quoted:

> The age of nations has passed. Now, unless we wish to perish we must shake off our old prejudices and build the earth. . . . The more scientifically I regard the world, the less can I see any possible biological future for it except the active consciousness of its unity.[28]

To reach the desired "higher plane of humanity" requires a complete change in people's "fundamental way of valuation and action." The earth "will only become conscious of itself through the crisis of conversion."[29] This leads to questions about the future of the spirit on earth, the further spiritual evolution of our planet, and of the role of religion within the human community in process of further unification. From the perspective of his Christian faith, which believers of other faiths might share, it is the function of religion "to sustain and spur on the progress of life,"[30] and this religious, or we might prefer to say spiritual, function grows in parallel with the growth of humans and the growth of the noosphere around the world.

3. Spiritual Energy Resources to Feed the Zest for Life and Advance Human Unity

An enormous number of material and spiritual resources (sometimes described as cultural and spiritual capital) are needed to ensure a viable future for humanity. Certain external and internal conditions have to be fulfilled if human and natural life is to remain in balance, and if these conditions are not met, life on earth will fail. Teilhard was well aware of our precarious situation, as clearly stated in his work *Man's Place in Nature*:

Should the planet become uninhabitable before mankind has reached maturity; should there be a premature lack of bread or essential metals; or, what would be still more serious, an insufficiency, either in quantity or quality, of cerebral matter needed to store, transmit, and increase the sum total of knowledge and aspirations that at any given moment make up the collective germ of the noosphere: should any of these conditions occur, then, there can be no doubt that it would mean the failure of life on earth; and the world's effort fully to centre upon itself could only be attempted again elsewhere. . . .[31]

The necessary internal conditions are linked to the full exercise of human freedom: "a *know-how to do*" to avoid various traps and blind alleys such as "politico-social mechanisation, administrative bottle-necks, over-population, counter-selections" and, most important "a *will to do*," not to opt out, not to be discouraged by difficulties or fears.[32] Teilhard often speaks about the need to examine all available energy resources, especially those required for nourishing and sustaining human growth and action. A nuanced treatment of this theme is found in his important 1937 essay "Human Energy."[33] Central to maintaining the dynamic of action is the zest for life, the will to live and love of life—indispensable for the continuity and the development of a higher life. Teilhard warned that the chief enemies are indifference and boredom, the loss of a taste for life, the absence of inner resources, and the danger of dropping out. As he pointed out:

. . . all over the earth the attention of thousands of engineers and economists is concentrated on the problem of world resources of coal, oil or uranium—and yet nobody . . . bothers to carry out a survey of the zest for life: to take its "temperature," to feed it, to look after it, and . . . to increase it.[34]

In looking at its resources, the human community does not give the same attention to its available spiritual energy resources as it does to the calculation of its available material energy reserves.

Yet spiritual energy resources are indispensable for sustaining persons and the planet. Human beings bear the responsibility to locate them, use them for their sustenance, and increase them. The religious and philosophical traditions of the world—our global religious heritage—contain irreplaceable resources on which we must draw to nourish our zest for life, sustain the biosphere, foster the growth of the noosphere, and advance the balanced integration of the diverse groups and nations of the global community. Nowhere is this better expressed than in Teilhard's 1950 address on "The Zest for Living" to the Congrès Universel des Croyants, mentioned earlier. At the deepest level, the zest for life is linked to an act of faith:

> . . . what is most vitally necessary to the thinking earth is a faith—and a great faith—and ever more faith.
>
> To know that we are not prisoners.
>
> To know that there is a way out, that there is air, and light and love, somewhere, beyond the reach of all death.
>
> To know this, to know that it is neither an illusion nor a fairy tale.
>
> That, if we are not to perish smothered in the very stuff of our being, is what we must at all costs secure.
>
> And it is there that we find what I may well be so bold as to call the *evolutionary role* of religions.[35]

Teilhard recognized the diversity and complementarity of what he called "the active currents of faiths," that is, the living religious traditions present in the world today. All religions are undergoing profound transformations under the impact of modernity and the exponential development of modern science and technology, but each of them still contains "fragments of vision" and bears witness to "experiences of contact" with a supreme Ineffable—elements that are most precious in feeding the zest for life. The global religious heritage of humankind contains spiritual resources that are "as indispensable and irreplaceable for the integrity of a total terrestrial religious consciousness as the various 'racial' components."[36] In developing this idea further, I suggest that similar to the way we are concerned about preserving the biodiversity of life forms, we need to take conscious account of, and responsibility for, maintaining the rich "noospheric" diversity of religious and spiritual ideas, since they provide us with irreplaceable resources for feeding the zest for life.

Teilhard de Chardin favored a closer contact and dialogue between members of different faiths, and encouraged their active collaboration in making the world a better place through promoting a greater integration of the diverse elements of humanity. He also stressed that contemporary religious needs are different from those in the past. Our consciousness and historically new situation require a new spirituality and a new image of God. A spirituality mainly concerned with the individual is no longer sufficient; what is needed is a faith in humanity and the earth. Teilhard's own spirituality was deeply rooted in what he called the *"divine milieu,"* a deep faith in a divine centre and heart of the world that suffuses every context and environment with the energy, presence, and grace of the spirit whose dynamic action animates the entire universe. Thus the noosphere is not only a sphere of human evolution, but one that bears the traces of divine love and transfiguration. Love is for him both a human task and an "effect of 'grace' and 'revelation.'"[37] To create stronger bonds within the human community and bring about a better world for all, the energies of love—the highest form of human energy—in all its different dimensions and practical expressions are what is needed most.

Conclusion

Teilhard de Chardin's vision for feeding "the zest for life" within ourselves and within the world is truly empowering and inspirational, if we really want to seed and grow a better future for the whole of humanity, and not only for its privileged members. There now exist a growing number of "noospheric institutions" which are working in many fields for the good of the inhabitants of the earth. New processes of global networking are constantly emerging, and the possibilities for a "global-interlinking-through-love," that Teilhard first perceived in the 1930s, have grown exponentially through the fast advances of electronic means of communication. Nowhere is this more evident than in the global aid efforts for the victims of the recent tsunami disaster in Asia. Is this only a passing event soon to be forgotten again, or will it serve as an inspiring example for future collaboration on planet Earth? We need more such global cooperation to also help the victims of the Iraqi war and the Sudanese famine, for transcending numerous forms of deeply engrained violence, human rights abuses, and for healing the lethal scars of war and hatred.

Traditional religions, spiritualities, and ethics provide irreplaceable resources to help our thinking and decision making, but they are not ready-made blueprints. We need both ancient and modern streams of wisdom to effect the planetary transformation and renewal we seek. Thomas Berry has explained this so well in his challenging book *The Great Work*,[38] where he lists, besides the wisdom resources of the classical religious and philosophical traditions, those of native traditions, the newly discovered wisdom of women and, interestingly, also the new wisdom of science. There is no shortage of spiritual energy resources, of inspiring visions and ideals, of pioneering groups and movements in the world today, yet it is also true that we still have to reap the benefits of these ideas and emergent practices, for so many hopes, visions, and ideals have yet to translate into concrete transformations in the lives of the poor and the oppressed. The significance and transformative potential of our visions and hopes for the future of humanity is immense. Their practical realization is so often still opposed by violent and powerful political and economic forces, which have to be strongly counteracted and fought against.

At the present critical stage of the world we have to pay attention to the deep need for spiritual well-being beyond the existing physical, mental, and moral needs of humankind. This was already recognized long ago by former United Nations Secretary-General U Thant and former Assistant Secretary-General Robert Muller, who reflected on the place of spirituality in secular society in his book *New Genesis: Shaping Global Spirituality*.[39] Today we hear much about development, but this is mostly understood in material and economic terms. It is seen as a problem of wealth and justice, as the distribution of resources and the balance of power. Teilhard was asking for more than that when he asked how deeply have we thought of the spiritual dimensions and the spiritual energy resources available for the further development of persons and planet. Will questions of spiritual development one day become an integral part of our efforts to ensure global developments toward peace and justice? What efforts are currently being devoted toward developing the inner resources of human beings: their power to love, care, and be compassionate, as well as their ability to be peaceful and happy, so that we can ensure the growth of human flourishing for all peoples in the world? What the world needs most of all is a new global order and a new global ethics on whose fundamentals we can begin to agree. How much could be achieved, for example, if all Muslims and Christians in the world, who represent half the global population, worked closely together for the well-being of the whole human community.

In order to change our world we have to foster the resolve, the commitment, and the will to change our ways. Only then can we create a new global order animated by a different and new spirit. This will not be possible without a spiritual renewal, a return to the values of life, and a common commitment to a qualitatively better life for all. Religious and spiritual renewal is now occurring in a secular, pluralistic context, and religions must relate and speak to that context too.

Tremendous spiritual energy resources exist in each faith tradition and in many other sources of wisdom we possess. We can draw on all these as never before, and these resources can help us in developing more harmonious relations between humans, the earth and our cosmic environment. We can also find many seeds for peace-making in the world's religions, but at the same time we need to recognize and address the existing seeds of violence and hatred. To transform our planet from one of dissension and disorder, from war, violence and strife, and the likelihood of eco-logical disaster, into one of peaceful co-existence, does mean a change of heads and hearts. At present we have a world more torn apart than ever before, yet it is also a world that is longing to be one. The widespread public desire for closer collaboration and for a more just and peaceful world, among so many people around the globe today, may be well ahead of the thinking and planning of many national governments.

As Teilhard de Chardin wrote long ago in *The Human Phenom-enon*, some elements of the world may well "refuse to serve the world"[40] at this critical time of its development, but if our vision and will can grow large and strong enough, we can find the neces-sary energy resources to feed the zest for life, and work together toward a more hopeful future for all of humanity.

CHAPTER 2

God and the Human Future
Thomas M. King, S.J.

Teilhard was in the midst of his Jesuit and scientific studies when, in late December of 1914, he was drafted into the French army. He was given three weeks of training and sent to the front lines of the First World War, as a stretcher-bearer. During the previous fifteen years he had lived in the quiet of a Jesuit community life. Suddenly he was thrown among strangers with different values and into the chaos of trench warfare. In this troubled situation he came to have an intensified sense of God and the human future. This is most evident in an essay written in 1917, "Nostalgia for the Front." Teilhard wrote this essay during a period of some days' rest from battle, and he expresses a yearning to be back in the action, for at the front he felt "elevated to the very frontier of the World—close to God."[1]

He recalled that, "during those days of unforgettable confusion—with clouds of dust everywhere and with all the shouting—when rations, flares and hand grenades were being chaotically distributed to those who were streaming up for the great offensive," he found "peace and exaltation in the superhuman atmosphere in which the soul had again become acclimatized."[2] It was there that he first could understand the human future: "A window was opened onto the hidden mechanisms and deep strata of what man is becoming."[3] When in mortal danger, he found the "light that danger kindles,"[4] and by that light he claimed humanity to be "born above all in hours of crisis."[5] In this essay, when Teilhard first refers to humanity as a higher reality, he calls it a "Thing,"—that is, in the French, *une Chose* with a capital *C*: "Another Thing lives in him and dominates him." But soon he goes beyond the impersonal Thing to speak of "a Personality of another order," and of a "Soul."[6]

1. Patriotism, Ideologies and Science Animating the World

I would like to develop two points from these passages in "Nostalgia for the Front." First, Teilhard becomes aware, in the crisis of battle, of "what man is becoming."At the battlefront, he saw himself "at the frontier of the world—close to God." Perhaps the best way to understand these passages is in terms of Teilhard's understanding of evolution. Evolution proceeds by groping—that is, it does not advance simply by chance, but by "directed chance."[7] The battlefield seemed to be the front of the living world; there, where life is largely a matter of chance, he encountered God giving direction to the future. After the quiet stability of Jesuit life, he was suddenly destabilized and found himself at the forefront of the world. There, danger and the divine Hand, chance and direction, were experienced together. There, "at the very frontier of the world—close to God," he could see the Promised Land. Teilhard writes, "It is only when danger threatens that the future can be seen by us distinctly. . . . Those who have not been within an inch of death have never really seen what lay ahead of them."[8] Danger reveals God and the future. When highly dependent on chance, we find the divine hand directing evolution. Consequently, during the war he was both a risk-taker and more deeply religious than before. Throughout his life, he remained a risk-taker, perhaps in order to feel close to God and be better able to see where humanity was going.

The second point has to do with the sequence in which Teilhard knows "another Thing that lives in him," "some human essence higher than himself,"[9] and then soon after switches from the impersonal terms and speaks of it as a "new and superhuman soul,"[10] a "personality of another order." Later, in writing *The Phenomenon of Man*, he presented the same sequence: First he tells of a new reality that has great power, and calls it an "unnamed Thing," or "the great Thing that had to come,"[11] then he argues that the Thing must be hyperpersonal, and calls it a "Soul"[12]— something more than a Thing. Yet in both "Nostalgia" and *The Phenomenon of Man* this higher reality is first presented as a Thing, for that is how the higher reality is first known. Many soldiers knew this higher Thing as "France," as a future ideal for which they were willing to die. Teilhard writes of standing next to a soldier in the trench who called out "Pour la France," before leaping out of the trench and running toward the German lines, only to be shot down. France was the *Thing* that seemed to animate his brave deed. Many in the twentieth century extended the ideal and spoke of the ideal as "Humanity." Teilhard did too, but he went beyond such "Things" to speak of a divine Soul, a personal Someone.

In the century just passed, notions for the future of Humanity motivated many idealistic people. This future was most forcefully articulated by the Marxists. In the 1930s millions dedicated themselves with "religious devotion" to the communist goal. Teilhard told of an "immediate sympathy and profound agreement" with these "emancipated servants of the earth." He was beguiled by their vision, but was soon disappointed once he saw where their ideals led.[13] The Marxist future was an impersonal one that centered on an impersonal and depersonalizing ideal. This ideal led to the impersonal Soviet system and servitude. They had dedicated themselves to the future as an impersonal Thing.

Teilhard also identified with scientists, another group in which many were dedicated to the future of humanity; with them he sympathized, but he also disagreed with many of them. He objected that secular scientists act with reason and their senses, but never with their hearts. This can lead to the scientist who works like a drone on a work that dehumanizes him; in some sense he has given himself to the human task, but to do so has rendered the self less than human.[14] Teilhard argues that if these scientists could believe in a future with a soul, what a difference it would make. Everything leading to that soul would be "warmed, illumined and animated, and consequently becomes an object to which one gives one's whole adhesion."[15] He claims those people who are able to follow this course are able to love the lowest of their tasks as passionately as if they could caress it. Their work does not consume them, rather it is a communion with the personal God who is present in all they touch.

2. *The Higher Soul Animating Us*

This higher soul can be defined in the claim of St. Paul: "I live, no longer I, but Christ lives in me" (Gal 2:20). In a true sense Paul identified with his own human soul, so he says: "*I* live." His soul animated his body, but beyond this Paul tells of being animated by Christ, a higher soul within him. The Latin word for soul is "*anima*" and the soul is seen as "animating" the body. If we do not know this higher soul, we find all our actions leave us divided. We most often act only from a tiny portion of ourselves. Whether eating or working, or doing mathematics or a crossword puzzle, man is only partially engaged in his activity, with only one or another of his faculties. His senses, or his limbs, or his reason function, but never his heart itself: human action, but not the action of a whole man, as the scholastics would say. That is why after a life of highest effort, a scientist or a thinker may end up impoverished, desiccated, and disillusioned; his mind but not his personality has worked on inanimate objects. He has given himself, but he has not been able to love.[16]

Teilhard sees us as divided between seeing and thinking, between understanding and loving, between living and dying. But if we know we are animated by this great soul, seeing and thinking, understanding and loving, living and dying involve us completely; we are wholly involved in what we do. Teilhard says Christianity "sur-animates; hence it introduces a higher principle of unity into our spiritual life."[17] But the higher soul is also found in the material with which the scientist works. When one is aware of the personal soul that is coming into being, everything appears sacred. In this lies Teilhard's appreciation of the environment and the respect we owe to it. There is no longer the depersonalized world that has been central to much scientific work. If the philosophy of the environmentalist allows only a depersonalized world, it is difficult to see why such a world should be valued.

Teilhard would speak of this higher soul as the world soul, and see it "sur-animating" (or super-animating) all of us and making us one. So, he affirms, Christianity should not be seen as an added burden, it is "a Soul of immense power which bestows significance and beauty" on our lives.[18] To understand this super-soul we might imagine a cell that has been removed from a body. It can continue living apart from me, but when it is restored to my body it would have the sense of a higher soul, our human soul, our self, animating it. If the cell were originally mine, then as it was again incorporated into my body it could say (in imitation of St. Paul), "I live, now not, but Tom King lives in me." It would still have its own life, but I would be sur-animating it. In me the cell would be able to do things that it could not do on its own. This is one of the things that happens to us when we are taken into omega, the higher soul: We lead a wider life and gain a vitality that amazes us. Some people can get such a feeling if they are brought into a wider unit, such as "the nation." But large organizations can depersonalize those who serve them. This would not happen if the unifying element were a soul, and not simply a Thing.

In the context of receiving a higher animation—animated by a higher soul—an essay that Teilhard wrote years before the First World War has especial relevance. In November of 1908 Teilhard began studies in theology in England. He was asked by the editors of *Études* (a theological journal edited by the French Jesuits) to write an article on the healings at Lourdes. He interviewed two medical doctors in Paris: One had just finished a thesis on the healings, and the other was Director of Medical Verification at the shrine. The article appeared in *Études* the following January, under the title "The Miracles at Lourdes and the Canonical Investigations."

At the time, many secular voices dismissed the healings as "hysteria," or "religious suggestion." Teilhard's feeling was that these secular people had confined themselves to their own narrow philosophies and were unwilling to acknowledge the "extra-medical facts" that did not fit their theories. He urged that those who had written criticisms of Lourdes, such as Emile Zola, should go to Lourdes and study the records, as several well-substantiated and rapid cures had been documented. Teilhard wrote of "an other who works . . . and this mysterious other can be none other than God." However, he pointed out that the miracles at Lourdes[19] involved no violation of the laws of nature. He noted that the healings were striking, but that they were all limited in the sense that there had been nothing so radical as the raising of a dead man to life, or accounts of missing limbs being miraculously restored.

Teilhard would pick up this theme again in 1920 when he wrote of God acting on us like a soul of the world. It is in this context that he would write of miracles (such as at Lourdes) as extensions of biology.[20] But what is meant by a miracle that extends biology and does not violate the laws of nature? God acts within us as a higher soul. We are like those cells from my body which can be kept alive artificially outside my body. When they return to my body they gain a new vitality and become part of my acts; they can do things they could not do apart from me, but there is no violation of the laws on nature. In the same way, Teilhard claimed we can do new and wondrous things when we are integrated into the body of Christ: Then we can feel the higher life in our selves. Believers find their spirits are raised and they can even find they are physically healed. But there is no violation of the laws of nature; the higher soul is working within them; it is sur-animating them.

3. *The Belief in the Human Future and in a Personal God*

Like "Nostalgia for the Front," Teilhard's *Phenomenon of Man* is concerned with a higher *Thing* and later refers to the same reality as a higher *Soul*. This soul, which now is animating humanity, has been animating all life down through the millennia. It is caring for us and for this planet in a personal (or supra-personal) way. In *The Phenomenon of Man* Teilhard expresses his concern about the future of the planet, yet reassures the reader by looking to the past: "In bringing us into existence it [the planet] has juggled miraculously with too many improbabilities for there to be any risk whatever in following it right to the end."[21] The passage suggests God is personally involved with the planet's life. Again in the same work, he describes those who fear that a comet could strike the earth and eliminate all life. This had been suggested in the French Enlightenment and caused Denis Diderot great concern. In much the same manner, today some contemporary science fiction writers conceive of a disaster that might eliminate life as we know it. Teilhard suggested several possible disasters that might occur and allowed such an end is theoretically possible, but added, "We have higher reasons for being sure, that *they will not happen*"—the final phrase is in italics. Why will they not happen? He answers, there is "a secret complicity between the infinite and the infinitesimal (*de l'Immense et de l'Infime*) to warm, nourish, and sustain us."[22] This can only mean that the infinite God is taking a personal care of us. A striking claim that has not received much attention! This personal care describes the difference between having a personal soul for the human future and having only an impersonal Thing.

Teilhard further believed that this soul had a personal interest in him and others. Upon receiving his doctorate he reflected, "All takes place before me and within me with a palpable solicitude of events."[23] While on his first expedition in China he wrote, "During the last two months we could not go where we wanted [because of bandits], and found something [of scientific interest] everywhere. I believe the Lord leads us."[24] In Java, after a significant fossil had been found there, he asked, "What did they mean, these successive strokes of good luck? What is God asking of me?" But he believed others were also led by a personal Providence, so he wrote to a non-believing friend: "May life become for you not just some blind favorable fatality, but a kind of living Presence or Benevolence in which it will be possible for you not only to trust, but to confide."[25]

Teilhard felt it was only in a situation of great instability that one is able to see the Promised Land. At the frontier of the human wave, he felt close to where God was shaping the human future. Joseph Pieper, a leading Catholic philosopher of the twentieth century, said it is only during the existential disturbances of love or death that we can see beyond the commonplace and write significant philosophy, poetry, or prayer.[26] In the war, Teilhard knew the existential disturbances of both love and death and this enabled him to see beyond the commonplace. In those troubled times, Teilhard's ideas first came to him as a passionate vision, and only later did they became a philosophy. He would nuance his claims in the years to come, but the vision was antecedent to the philosophy.

In several places Teilhard speaks of this higher identity as a soul and not a Thing. That is, as a personal God and not just an impersonal humanity. Yet it first presented itself to him as a Thing, that is, as "France," as the "Allies," as "Humanity," etc., an identity greater than one's individual self. Sometimes, in order to reach a wider audience, the followers of Teilhard have set aside mention of a personal God. That is a good way of beginning to speak of Teilhard, but in leaving it there one would miss a highly significant part of what he had to tell us. That is, through the higher soul our work will not depersonalize us, religion will become more prevalent, and because of "a secret complicity" between ourselves and God, humans can rest assured *there will be a human future.*

CHAPTER 3

The Personalization of the Universe; or, The Era of the Person

Henri Madelin, S.J.

Teilard de Chardin did not use the word "globalization" when he wrote about the future of humanity. His vision is neither a utilitarian nor a quietist one, based on renunciation, nor is it full of an exacerbated form of piety. It is centered on a Christic perspective that accompanies evolution from the beginning to the end. From inchoative matter to the noosphere, the Spirit draws all forward. A goal of "amorization" emerges and grows in the heart of matter itself. *Amorization* is a word derived from the Latin, which can be understood as an ever-increasing openness to "the other," in the entire scale of being. It is a concept that implies a movement from a merely exterior to an interior relationship with other beings and entities: from the dominance of instinct to relationship with others, from the struggle for self-preservation to a growth in capacity for love. A final focusing is in the making, the famous "omega point."

Teilhard wrote in the singular, referring to a single person to differentiate from "massification," or confusion in anonymity. He described a process that brings about "personalization" and respect for each individual. But the adventure may fail if humans retreat into a kind of frozen self-absorption and are no longer stimulated and motivated to grow. Teilhard hoped that humanity would converge so that little by little it would meet the ultimate goal: resolving differences so as to succeed in bringing about a more humane existence. Teilhard wrote, "Matter, the matrix of the Spirit. The Spirit, a higher state of Matter"[1]—these are concepts that are central to his thought.

1. A Growing Humanity

The experience of the 1914–18 war was decisive for Teilhard, and where he came to know an intense sensation of freedom, the headiness of brotherhood, and the loss of earlier certitudes that were too simple. Teilhard always kept a certain nostalgia for this confrontation with death which was experienced simultaneously with an affirming liberty.

1. The Atmosphere on the Front

Teilhard had written for the Jesuit review *Études* (November 1917) about this "nostalgia for the front." Later, in "The Heart of The Matter," he returned to the atmosphere he found there, where millions of men gathered together developed an "internal energy" bringing about the raising of its "psychic temperature." A new sense emerged:

> Is it not for having been immersed—for being permeated month after month—exactly there where it was at its highest charge, its highest density that decidedly I ceased to make out any rupture between all things "physical" or "moral," "natural" or "artificial," (if not any differences): the "Million Men" with its psychic temperature and its internal energy became for me a notion whose evolution was as real, biologically speaking, as that of

a gigantic protein molecule. Following this I have often been surprised to see around me, in my opponents, a complete inability to conceive that the human individual, as he represents a corpuscular notion, must, just like any other corpuscular species in the World, become engaged in links and physical groups that are superior to him, groupings that he cannot understand directly as such—because they are of an $n + 1$ order—but whose existence and whose influence are well known to him, through different pieces of evidence. This gift, or faculty, still rather rare, of being able to perceive without seeing the reality and the organicity of collective concepts is indubitably, I must repeat, due to the experience of the Great War, which allowed me to become aware of it and develop it in me as another sense.[2]

2. *An Ultimate Envelope*

As the war experience subsided, Teilhard became certain that an "envelope" exists, that is both conscious and thinking: "Not only did I no longer harbor any difficulty in understanding, in an intuitive way, the organic unity of the living membrane, spread like a film over the illuminated surface of the star that carries us. But also, in an individualizing process, detaching itself little by little, like a luminous aura, all around this sensitive protoplasmic layer, an ultimate envelope began to appear to me—not only a conscious envelope but a thinking one—where henceforth it would no longer cease to concentrate itself, to my eyes, with a brilliance and growing consistency: the essence, or better still, the Soul of the Earth."[3]

It was relatively late that Teilhard gave the name "noosphere" to this layer of thought that covers the earth. It developed at a great pace in the modern world, because of the globalization of communication, and the speed in which people can now move quickly to any part of the inhabited world. Researchers and scientists discuss their hypothesis and compare their solutions, nourished by one another's ideas. Each one can then enlarge the content of his knowledge on any topic. Through the media one can, without ever leaving home, be knowledgeable about current events, discoveries, and initiatives which happen a thousand miles away. The earth, as Teilhard stressed, has become too small, and it is now interstellar space that keeps our minds busy.

The many thoughts communicating and mutually fertilizing each other are all part of the new sphere. Our new partners in the exchange would have been ignored in the world we are now leaving. This new sphere, impregnated by spirit, is completely intertwined in the material world. It is like a thin skin completely attached to the matter which has engendered us in a world of communicating spirits. The human species has ceased to evolve biologically, but does not stop growing in this "spiritual" trade which is now our destiny.

3. The Feminine "Materia Matrix"

In an essay written on October 30th, 1950, near the end of his life, Father Teilhard returned to the subject of the feminine in the noosphere's universe, situated at the junction between the cosmic sense and the human sense. To arrive at this idea he had to reject old social and religious molds. He made two assertions that confirm this breakthrough, the fruit of his maturity. "No more than light, oxygen or vitamins can man—any man—go without the feminine (an obvious fact that grows truer every day)."[4] Outside of marriage, too narrowly focused, in society, on reproduction, and the religious life, presented as a theological necessity for a kind of separatism, a third way exists that renders necessary the transformation of the concept of "spirit." This concept consists of a spirit that is not dematerialized but is a synthesis, a *materia matrix*. Not a fleeing from (by re-entrenchment) but a conquest (by sublimation) of unfathomable spiritual forces yet drugged by the mutual attraction of the sexes. It is a task for chastity, still to come. It is not "the step to "amorization" but the central person-to-person inflammation. After the coming of the reflexive monad one beholds the formation of the affective dyad where a living spark is produced and with it the formation of the unifying cement of the world, represented by the "feminine Universal."

Teilhard predicted that chastity could now be lived in a less frozen mode, more open to complementary relationships between the genders, as referred to in the story of Genesis. It should no longer be the exclusive domain of the monastic person who has taken a vow. It cannot be conceived anymore as an avoiding, an abstention, but as a communion of a new type, in view of a better realization of the specific capacities of men and women. Chastity should now be a call also for bachelors and married couples. Schools are now largely co-ed. In many countries of the world, despite the resistance from those concerned with religious and cultural traditions, women no longer agree to being relegated to subordinate positions or chained to domestic tasks. They aspire to escape the holy trinity of tasks which were assigned to them in the past: the children, the kitchen, the church ("Kinder, Küche, Kirche"). The affective life and children's upbringing should not confine women to conventional positions, since their potential in many other fields remains immense. Religious celibacy is rejuvenated if it leads to the recognition that frequent contact with the other sex can bring personal development. Better control of the primary instincts and the sublimation of sexuality should allow the men and women of our times to be less dependent on a sexuality which up to now has been too exclusively oriented toward reproduction.

The experience of the war, the awareness of the communication of thoughts and the encounter with the feminine were the cradle in which Teilhard envisioned the growth of humanity. The essays and correspondence written during the long years he spent in Beijing point out that for Father Teilhard: "a universe of personal fabric" and a universe "with a converging curve" come to mean "the same." It is the "only milieu able to give both Christ whom we adore, to receive him, and man whom we dream of, to take interest in him."[5]

2. *The Possible Failure of Humanity*

The personalization of the world may fail if egotism and individualism result rather than a respect for differences. If the economics and politics of nations are motivated by these baser instincts, then the standards of behavior will not be up to what they should be, considering what is at stake today. "The Human Phenomenon," published in 1930 in Louvain's *Revue des questions scientifiques*, demonstrates that the failure of this personalization of the world is an eventuality for Teilhard.[6] His doubts began during the 1929 world economic crisis.

Life, a path or a dead-end? This is the question, scarcely asked over the centuries, that is today on the lips of humanity's masses. After the short and violent crisis when humanity became aware simultaneously of its creative powers and faculties of thought, humanity became legitimately difficult; and no urge of the instincts or blind economic need will be enough to make it advance. Only one, true and important reason can be behind the impetus to push life further on, and that is to passionately love life. But where can we find, on an experimental level, the beginning (if not the completion) of something that justifies Life? Nowhere else, it seems, than when considering the intrinsic value of the human phenomenon.

If you consider Man as an accidental addition, or a plaything among many other things, you will lead him to such disgust and revolt that if this was generalized, it would mark the end of Life on Earth. Admit, on the other hand, that in our experience, Man, because he is on the breast of the two vast waves in which, for us, tangible Reality divides itself, holds in his hands the fortune of the Universe: and he will turn to face a grand sunrise.

Man is allowed to worry about himself when he feels lost, isolated in the mass of things. But he may joyfully continue on his way when he realizes that his fate is the same as Nature's. Because then it would no longer be considered a virtue for him, but rather a spiritual illness, to question the value and the hopes of a world.[7]

Besides being a Jesuit priest, Teilhard de Chardin was also a man of science. His faith and his conception of the world were always in accordance with one another. In 1942 he wrote, in "Being More," "Imagining any discordance between God and human progress will undermine the faithful, and close the door to the faith for those who do not believe."[8]

However, Pierre Teilhard did not ignore the possibility of God's withdrawal and the possibility of the failure of a human evolution that had become conscious of itself. In 1930, as if he were seized by vertigo, the Christian scholar was in doubt, as we have just seen. He wondered if humanity, like a race horse approaching a frightening hurdle, would refuse to jump over the obstacle and take refuge in a whirlwind of ancestral fears. The problem was not only the economic crisis of 1929, but also the conjunction, in the heart of the new humanity, of "its creative power and its faculties for criticism." The specter of nihilism still haunts the mind. More than ever before, humanity has today "become legitimately difficult." A huge question grows in the heart and on the lips of the human masses: Is life a path or a dead-end?

The answers can no longer come from traditional sources. Neither the mechanism of "instincts" nor "blind economic needs" can make the human caravan advance. These urges are not strong enough when faced with new mentalities. Today's situation has been defined by the abrupt affirmation: Yesterday I was hungry, today I am afraid. Humans today may feel with reason that they are "isolated in the mass of things." One can add that the uncertainty about the origins of humans, and science's developments in regard to human's animality, can instill doubts as to the originality of the human phenomenon as it is considered in the milling swarms of the biosphere. If man is seen as "an accidental addition or as a plaything" the strings of his joy of life may break. This would lead to the "definitive failure of life on earth."[9]

Only a passionate love of life can push man to "go further on" in time and space. Going over and over one's past is not important. It is advisable to turn one's "face to the rising sun." The terminal point, the omega point, is the same for this Christian scholar as those Fathers of the Church who sung of the ultimate divinization of man by and in Christ.

Pierre Teilhard was aware that many would see only a pipe dream in this vision of a magnificent future. But he took care of this objection in advance as he wrote: "Let us admit that it is a dream; we should like to follow it to its end, this dream, and see how the immensity and the depth of the World are even more harmonious in our reveries, than in the narrow reality one would wish to retain us in."

3. The Era of the Person

"Under the influence of solitary egotisms," the universe is exposed to the risk of disintegration, and we must seriously consider the eventual discouragement of the human spirit. Father Teilhard believed in the possibility of a faltering of the human adventure due to a lack of motivation and the abdication of our freedom. But he also knew that humans are given choice, and so believed that with this liberty people would opt for the survival of humanity, and the growth of sense and solidarity as they become more conscious than before of their responsibilities.

1. Union and Differentiation

In "The Grand Option," a text written on March 3rd 1939, Teilhard wrote of the properties of union:

> It is at this point that we must rid ourselves of a prejudice which is deeply embedded in our thought, namely the habit of mind which causes us to contrast unity with plurality, the element with the whole, and the individual with the collective, as though these were diametrically opposed ideas. We constantly argue as though in each case the terms varied inversely, a gain on the one side

being ipso facto the other side's loss; and this in turn leads to the widespread idea that any destiny on 'monist' lines would exact the sacrifice and bring about the destruction of all personal values in the Universe.

The origin of this prejudice, which is largely imaginary, can no doubt be traced to the disagreeable sense of loss and constraint which the individual experiences when he finds himself involved in a group or lost in a crowd. It is certainly the case that any agglomeration tends to stifle and neutralize the elements which compose it; but why should we look for a model of collectivity in what is no more than an aggregate, a "heap"? Alongside these massive inorganic groupings in which the elements intermingle and drown, or more exactly at the opposite pole to them, Nature shows herself to be full of associations brought about and organically ordered by a precisely opposite law. In the case of associations of this kind (the only true and natural associations) the coming together of the separate elements does nothing to eliminate their differences. On the contrary, it exalts them. In every practical sphere true union (that is to say, synthesis) does not confound; it differentiates. This is what it is essential for us to understand at the moment of encountering the Grand Option.[10]

As Father Teilhard writes in "The Human Phenomenon," convergence does not mean confusion: "Just as the meridians approach the pole, science, philosophy and religion are bound to converge as they draw nearer to the whole. They converge, I say; but do not merge, and constantly continue to attack Reality under numerous angles and planes."[11]

2. *Philosophical Readjustment*

The historical tendency of human constructive action has been to globally orient itself in a direction that could satisfy its aspirations for all forms of greater consciousness. If this were the historical choice of successive individuals, one could conclude that the "Grand Option," the option that chooses a converging universe, would sooner or later become the shared option of the human masses. This would necessarily change the lines of reality that surround us. Because "to philosophize," for Teilhard, "is to put in order the lines of reality around us." We are therefore going to witness an evolution of the space in which our ideas are made:

> The historians of philosophy, in their study of the development of thought through the ages, prefer to dwell upon the birth and evolution of ideas, thesis, and formally constructed systems. But arguable schemes of this sort do not constitute the whole, or perhaps even the most important part, of the life of the spirit. A geometrical system is made up of points, lines and diagrams. But in the deeper sense it depends on the type of space (number of dimensions, curvature) in which the system operates. According to the nature of this space properties change or are generalized and certain transformations and movements become possible. Space in itself is something that overflows any formula. Yet it is in terms of this inexpressible that a whole expressible world is interpreted and developed. Well! What is true and clearly apparent in the abstract field of geometry may also be found, and should be examined with no less care, in the general systematization of phenomena which we call philosophy. To philosophize is to put in order the lines of reality around us. What first emerges from any philosophy is a coherent whole of harmonized relationships. But this whole, if we look closely, is always intuitively conceived in terms of a Universe endowed with certain fixed properties which are not a thing in themselves but *a general condition of knowledge*. If these properties should change, the whole philosophy, without necessarily breaking down, must adapt itself and readjust the relation between its parts; like a design on a sheet of paper which undergoes modification when the paper is curved. Indeed the past history of human intelligence is full of "mutations" of this kind, more or less abrupt, indicating, in addition to the shift of human ideas, an evolution of the "space" in which the ideas took shape—which is clearly very much more suggestive and profound.[12]

Conclusion

In a letter written in 1917, Teilhard wrote: "My calling has never seemed simpler nor clearer to me: to personalize the world in God."[13] As he was commenting on the works of his friend, Father de Lubac wrote: "In Father Teihard de Chardin's eyes a double victory was certain. The first was the victory of the Spirit on Matter. The Spirit is born in the World with Man, and will never perish."[14]

Father de Lubac then quoted Teilhard: "Whatever the unstable appearance of life, whatever its impressive links with the limiting spaces and destructive forces, one thing is more certain than all the rest because it is as certain as the World: The Spirit will always manage to foil all determinisms and hazards just as it has always done. It represents the indestructible part of the Universe."[15] "The descending wave of Entropy" will be beaten by the "'high tides' of the Noogenesis."[16] This evolution is irreversible. "The noosphere's temperature is constantly rising," or, in other words, "an intensification of consciousness" is occuring. The Universe is becoming personalized. Everything rises towards a "definitive summit."[17]

Father de Lubac concludes:

> Grafting itself on this first victory, which is necessary to its coming about, the second victory is no less assured: the victory of Christ, risen from the dead, whose pleroma will be accomplished one day; and through it, the self-confidence we gain from our faith, although it allows the subsistence, on their level, of all the human condition's worries, that reinforces and guarantees our belief in the victory of the Spirit. The "biological success" of Man can therefore never be for a Christian a simple probability: it is an absolute certainty.[18]

Translated by Anne Mortureux

Teilhard and Ecology

CHAPTER 4

Zest for Life: Teilhard's Cosmological Vision

Mary Evelyn Tucker

The multiple and interconnected human and environmental crises we face are of considerable urgency. As the world becomes warmer, as hurricanes increase, as species become extinct, as air and water pollution spreads, and as resource wars heat up, there is a disturbing sense among many environmentalists and ordinary citizens that the clock is ticking toward major disasters ahead. The looming planetary crisis, in its massive scale and increasing complexity, defies easy solutions. Moreover, the heightened frenzy of the global war on terrorism creates blindness toward the widespread terror humans have unleashed on the planet—on its ecosystems on land and in the oceans and on all the species they contain. Blindness is combined with enormous apathy or denial from various quarters regarding the scale of the problems we are facing.

Our withering planet requires sustained commitment to protection and restoration, but we in the "developed" world are easily distracted from these tasks by mass consumerism, media entertainment, and political manipulation. The fact that we are living in the midst of a period of mass extinction of species, caused by our plundering of Earth, is almost invisible to the majority of people in the world, who are simply going about the business of feeding their families or, in affluent regions, are acquiring more goods. A major wake-up call from our slumbering is required.

A vision for building a vibrant Earth community is needed. Life in all of its variety and beauty calls to us for a response, for the Earth's ecosystems are being rapidly destroyed in the name of progress and development. And this response requires not simply another managerial or legislative environmental plan for saving forests or fisheries, as important as these are. Rather, a new, integrated understanding and vision of who we are as humans is also essential. This is not just about stewardship of the Earth, but it is also about embracing our embeddedness in nature in radical, fresh, and enlivening ways. The younger generation, in particular, is searching for a means to understand its participatory role in nature and thus contribute to shaping a positive future.

Our challenge, then, is to identify the kind of vision which will spark the transformation that will create a multiform planetary civilization. This vision needs to evoke the values of empathy, compassion, and a sacrifice that has the welfare of future generations in mind. It needs especially to provide inspiration for human action—the great work, as Thomas Berry describes it. We are called, for the first time in history, to a new intergenerational consciousness and conscience that extends to the entire Earth community.

This is where Teilhard's vision of evolution can make a distinctive contribution to the emerging intersection of cosmology and ecology,[1] for Teilhard gives us an enlarged evolutionary context from which to understand our present human impact on the planet. As modern cosmology develops, Teilhard helps us to see the universe as an unfolding story; and as a modern ecology emerges Teilhard provides a profound understanding of relationality and interdependence. He evokes a vision of zest for the action needed to address the looming environmental and social problems of the 21st century. He points the way beyond doubt, indifference, and despair. He does this with a realistic but hopeful view of the beauty and complexity of the emergence of the universe along with a realization of our intimate connection with and dependence on all life forms. Thus, while Teilhard was not aware of the scale of the environmental crisis we are now facing, his powerful narrative of evolution provides the basis for an integrated ecological sensibility. His understanding of the role of humans within the context of evolution gives a framework for inspiring human action in various ways:

1. *Suffering and Loss.* Teilhard brings to us a sense of the ability to deal with the enormous suffering of our historical moment, filled as it is with destruction and despair.

2. *Cosmic Sense.* He gives us a superb sense of the cosmos as a context for our being and our becoming.

3. *The Within of Things.* The interiority of matter is a basis for communion with the universe and the Earth.

4. *Cosmogenesis.* He sees evolution as a dynamic, unfolding, creative process.

5. *The Zest for Life.* The sweep of cosmogenesis provides for Teilhard an enormous sense of joy; for we are participating in a universe that is filled with interiority, spontaneity, and creativity.

6. *Communion with Life.* Teilhard has identified the profound continuity of humans with the Earth so that our communion with life can be seen as a primary dimension of our very being. This integrated cosmological vision is an enlivening basis for an ecological understanding of our species identity.

1. Suffering and Loss

We live in a radically different world from the early twentieth century when Teilhard came of age. The arc of his life stretched across a century of such upheaval and change that we are still reeling from the impact. Two world wars and dozens of other smaller wars have left their traumatic imprint on millions of human minds, buried now in the crevices of millions of human hearts. The effects of the bloodiest century in human history have spilled over into our new millennium.

Teilhard felt this trauma directly in his own experience in the First World War as a stretcher-bearer. Witnessing the enormous destruction of human life in the front lines gave rise in him an unshakeable sense of the sacrificial nature of the universe. The vicious quality of trench warfare is something we can only dimly imagine. Yet, it was from that experience that Teilhard's larger vision emerged. We glimpse this in his reflections on suffering, death, illness, and on diminishment. He did not wish to ignore these harsh realities or explain them away in conventional terms. Suffering for Teilhard was more than simply a redemptive act where things will be healed and made whole again. For Teilhard suffering was the very marrow of the universe. He writes:

> What a vast human suffering spreads over the entire earth at every moment! Of what is this mass formed? Of blackness, gaps and rejections? No let me repeat, of potential energy. In suffering the ascending force of the world is concentrated in a very intense form. The whole question is how to liberate it and give it a consciousness of its significance and potentialities."[2]

Suffering for Teilhard was a source of potential energy. It was part of the transience of things, the decay of life, and the inevitable diminishment that holds us back and yet provides the grace for new energy to emerge. He observed this transience at an early age—in his hair being cut and thrown into the fire, in the rusting of iron, in the bittersweet experience of the passing of the seasons. He experienced the loss of several of his brothers and sisters at an early age, and he was deeply immersed in the ocean of pain, regret, and loss that many of us find ourselves in. He wrote letters of encouragement to his cousin who was an invalid. How to navigate across this immense sea of suffering was Teilhard's challenge to himself, and his search for an answer was his great gift to us. How to go forward in the midst of the anguish of life is a question that speaks powerfully to our present historical moment, when environmental crises threaten the very foundations of Earth's ecosystems.

Can we live with diminishment? Can we bear destruction? Can we hold the shards of our shattered world in our hearts even as those shards break us open? These were Teilhard's questions as much as they are ours. For what he pondered above all was the question of how a new vibrancy might flood into the human heart reeling from the aftermath of war in the 1920s, the economic depression of the 1930s, and the shadow of Hitler and fascism in the 1940s. What could provide a vivifying vision to respond to these upheavals and help to navigate a way forward? This was Teilhard's great challenge and one that he was preoccupied with his whole life as he struggled to articulate the human phenomenon as part of a universe story.

We need to remember the suffering that gave rise to his encompassing vision of an evolving universe—both personally in his own journey, and collectively in the upheavals of the first half of the 20th century—because that suffering spills over into our new millennium as we witness massive destruction of species along with the disintegration of social systems. Teilhard's cosmological perspective is one that can embrace our sense of loss, whether it is a parent we mourn, or a loved one, or an entire species, or ecosystem. Above all, in this world we inhabit, which is shedding its old forms and cracking open at the seams, it gives us a larger sense of unity and common destiny.

Our moment requires such a vivifying cosmological vision as he created. It demands an encompassing view of the whole of evolution—universe and Earth—so as to find the grounds of our participation in this process. This is the task of understanding and absorbing the new cosmological perspective that Teilhard has given us, along with other key scientists in the 20th century. The gift from these scientists was putting together a fuller understanding of the various chapters of evolution. Teilhard's contribution in particular is giving us the arc of the whole as well as the threads that weave it together. In Teilhard's hands these chapters become integrated, and a new unified cosmology begins to emerge. Fifty years later, we are celebrating the fruits of the seeds he planted in our attempts to understand and embrace the new cosmological story of the evolution of the universe.[3]

2. *Cosmic Sense*

This view of the whole is one of Teilhard's greatest contributions, something he calls the cosmic sense. He writes, "The cosmic sense must have been born as soon as humans found themselves facing the forest, the seas, and the stars. And since then we find evidence of it in all our experience of the great and unbounded: in art, poetry, in religion. Through it we react to the world as a whole as with our eyes to the light."[4]

I feel something of this cosmic sense amidst the redwoods in Muir woods in northern California. For amidst loss and suffering there is presence and mystery that draws us forward, that enchants us and allures us into a larger sense of drama and adventure.

Standing amidst the redwoods in Muir Woods I feel this presence and mystery. There is a grandeur here that is palpable. There is a silence here that is penetrating; there is depth that is endless. These ancient trees that cradle the western part of our North American continent hold within them the secrets of longevity, endurance, survival, and tenacity.

The light filters through the canopy, stretching to reach the forest floor. The immense presence of the trees, these sentinels of past eras, floods into one. They were present when the dinosaurs roamed. They witnessed their demise and the rise of early mammals and eventually the emergence of humans. These great silent presences draw us into vast sweeps of time and space—we feel the immensity of Earth's evolution here, we draw in the moist air breathed by earlier life forms, we wrap ourselves in the fog and mist that has kept these trees alive for millennia. We touch the soft red bark that protects the trees from insects with its acidic tannin. We walk across the roots intertwined with one another supporting trunks of massive heights. The canopy stretches beyond the reach of the naked eye into distant spaces.

Here we have a glimpse of life's ancient unfolding within that complex evolutionary process that Teilhard articulated so powerfully. Here is a window opening into the great sweep of life still present with us, from prehistoric ferns and redwoods to later mammals such as deer, squirrel, and fox. A presence that connects us to the cosmos is palpable here.

3. The Within of Things

What accounts for this feeling of presence in the redwoods? Teilhard would have explained it as the within of things. He writes:

> Indisputably, deep within ourselves, through a rent or tear, an "interior" appears at the heart of beings. This is enough to establish the existence of this interior in some degree or other everywhere forever in nature. Since the stuff of the universe has an internal face at one point in itself, its structure is necessarily *bifacial*; that is, in every region of time and space . . . *co-extensive with its outside, everything has an inside.*[5]

For Teilhard, the "heart of matter" is alive with an incandescent energy. We see this in his essay, "Spirit of the Earth," where he speaks of the human as the flame of a general fermentation of the universe. We observe this too in his "Mass on the World," where, without bread and wine in the remoteness of the Ordos Desert, he offers up all the elements of matter as the consecration of the Mass. For Teilhard, matter is not simply empty or one-dimensional dead materiality. All of matter has both a physical and psychic component and is infused with interiority and subjectivity.

This indispensable axiom of his thought has enormous implications.

Indeed, one might say that this is at the heart of the new understanding of cosmology that is emerging in our own times. Matter shines with inner radiance. We attune ourselves to this radiance as we open ourselves to the rich workings of matter and spirit, for we are made of the same substance. Our interior life arises out of the billions of years of the yearning of matter to open up the inner pulsations of life. From single cells to the redwoods is a journey of the unfolding of the interiority of matter. In this unfolding we discover that we are not isolated beings in a dead universe. Rather, we participate to the fullest degree in the vital presence of spirit coursing through matter.

We sense this in the presence of the redwoods—there is something more here than bark and branches, root and trunk, leaves and burls. There is the within of things that creates a vital community of life, breathing in the rich moisture from the ocean fog and drawing sunlight down to the fern-covered forest floor. All of this displays the power of the interiority of matter to develop, adapt, and sustain such a complex community of life. This unveiling of interiority is at the heart of matter moving through time, namely, cosmogenesis.

4. Cosmogenesis

In light of evolution, the universe is not simply a cosmos but a cosmogenesis. Teilhard sensed profoundly and poetically that evolution moved forward as a great cosmogenesis—an unfolding process of life-giving reality. No longer do we see the Earth as static, but as dynamic and changing, filled with potential to evolve over billions of years, to bring forth life forms, and to have humans dwell within life's systems. This discovery that we are part of developmental time changes human consciousness forever:

> For our age to have become conscious of evolution means
> something very different from and much more than having discov-
> ered one further fact, however massive and important that fact
> may be. It means (as happens with a child when he acquires the
> sense of perspective) that we have come alive to a new *dimension*.
> The idea of evolution is not, as sometimes said, a mere hypothesis,
> but a condition of all experience.[6]

For Teilhard evolution occurs as the unfolding of ever-greater
complexity and ever more intricate consciousness. The evolution
of our solar system, from the great flaring forth of the cosmos
13.7 billion years ago, to the emergence of galaxies and stars and
our planet Earth, was a journey of some 9 billion years. With each
step of the process, the particular conditions for life emerged. In
other words, cosmogenesis unfolds by means of the self-organizing dynamics of evolutionary processes. These self-organizing dynamics are evident across the sweep of evolution from stars and
galaxies to the emergence of life. They include such processes
within life as:

1. The membrane of a cell discerning when and how to let in
genetic material from another cell and then replicating itself.

2. The ovum choosing the sperm to fertilize the egg.

3. The multiple arrangements for finding food and for repro-
ducing among the winged, finned and furred forms of life.

All of these are examples of self-organizing dynamics that make
evolution possible. Thus we see cosmogenesis not just as an ema-
nation such as Plotinus imagined from the One flowing out to
form the many. Nor is it a great Chain of Being as the Western
medieval world envisioned, from simple life up to humans and
then to the Divine. Instead, Teilhard gives us a sense of an evolving developmental time of which we are a part. In this perspective,
evolution is seen as a nested community of life—emerging from
what came before, but becoming ever more complex and ever
more conscious.

5. *The Zest for Life*

How does this view of the transformations of the evolutionary processes relate to humans? For Teilhard it provides us with a deepening realization that all life forms arise out of these transforming processes and that they continue to energize us as humans. One of Teilhard's central aims was to provide an integrated view of human-Earth-universe relations so that humans would be engaged in action for the Earth community. This interest in the world and its future dynamics was critical to Teilhard, especially as he saw the disillusionment and despair that emerged in Europe as a result of the two world wars. For him the "taste for life" (*le goût de vie*) was vital to the animation of the human spirit. He was not interested in simply encouraging an otherworldly mysticism, but rather took great pleasure in discovering the divine within the rhythms of the world as expressed in evolution. He cultivated a sense of zest for life despite the challenges of several decades of exile from Europe while living in China, and despite not being allowed to publish his religious writings. No matter how much he suffered, from illness, loneliness, alienation, and failure, he tried to find the larger meaning and to rekindle the fires of joy.

Teilhard's capacity for a broad interest in the world was noteworthy. This was true for my father as well. The night before he had a stroke, seven years ago, we took a walk in the evening after dinner, as he liked to do. He spoke, as he often did, of how blessed we had been as a family and how important was our concern for those less fortunate. Although damaged in an earlier heart attack, his heart was still large enough to embrace the world with all of its attendant tragedies. My mother read him the newspaper each day right up until the end—he not flinching as so many do from the unnerving news that trails into our living rooms. For many our world is almost too much to bear, filled to overflowing with sad bad news. But he leaned forward in his chair, his right side frozen from the stroke, still eager somehow to know and love our world. This fascinates me because it suggests something of the taste for life remained right up to his death, enduring through a lifetime of challenges and persisting even through seven years of suffering from a stroke.

What is the root of that interest that could not be extinguished? How can we let the world in, especially when depression is so rampant in modern societies? How can we care about the world's future when fear of the future is widespread? How can we feel our actions will make a difference when human life and ecosystems are being diminished around the globe? Teilhard responded to this crushing of the human spirit by the destructive events of history with a vision of evolution that evokes in us a profound species identity—with the whole universe, and Earth evolution, and with all life forms. Humans arise from this dynamic unfolding process, we are part of it, and we participate in its future shaping. Herein lies an enormous potential for zest to be activated in our own time.

6. *Communion with Life*

In his book *The Evolving Self*, Mihaly Csikszentmihalyi acknowledges that our emerging consciousness as a planetary species in communion with other forms of life is vital to mutually enhancing human-Earth relations.

> The only value that all human beings can readily share is the continuation of life on earth. In this one goal all individual self-interests are united. Unless such a species identity takes precedence over the more particular identities of faith, nation, family, or person, it will be difficult to agree on the course that must be taken to guarantee our future. . . .[7]

Teilhard recognized that creating a species identity is the challenge of individuals as well as the Earth community. The future of evolution is at stake if we should fail. Csikszentmihalyi suggests:

It is for this reason that the fate of humanity in the next millennium depends so closely on the kind of selves we will succeed in creating. Evolution is by no means guaranteed. We have a chance of being part of it only as long as we understand our place in that gigantic field of force we call nature.[8]

One of the crucial areas we need to explore is the way in which our evolving selves are part of the larger matrix of life. How we commune with life will determine the future of other species and ecosystems. We can have a certain measure of confidence that we will arrive at a new season of our evolution as humans as we come to "understand our place within that vast field of force we call nature." It will be a season of freshness, as we rediscover the intertwined coding of ourselves as bio-cultural beings, and of the mixed heritage of biological survival and cultural creativity. This is the imperative of our evolution as a species that will require a new cultural coding resonant with, but distinguished from, the genetic coding of evolution itself. We can see ourselves now as imprinted with nature's complex coding and entwined within nature's rhythms. At the same time, our cultural coding needs to be brought into alignment with the forces and limits of nature. This will require new forms of education, religion, politics, law, and economics.

There are many indications that these forms are emerging and that we are evolving into our next phase as humans. With sustainable technologies and design, with ecological economics and politics, and with environmental education and ethics, we are learning how to assist evolution and to participate in the myriad processes of universe powers. If human decisions have swamped natural selection because of our planetary power as a species, we can learn how to become aligned again with a flourishing evolution. We will find the animating principles of universe evolution that also ground culture and guide humans in our creation of communities in what we protect, in what we build, in what we eat, and in what we cherish. We will become partners with evolutionary processes and in doing this rediscover our species identity. This is what Teilhard spoke of as hominization of the human and the planetization of life.

Conclusion

It was Teilhard's deepest desire that human action could be directed toward the planetization of life. He hoped that our presence within the biosphere of the planet would contribute to the enhancement of the Earth community. This would bring energy and zest to the human endeavor. He realized that at the same time as we are looking for new sources of physical energy, so too are we seeking the wellsprings of spiritual energy and motivation. In this vein he writes:

> If each of us can believe that he is working so that the Universe may be raised, in and through him, to a higher level—then a new spring of energy will well forth in the heart of Earth's workers. . . . Indeed, the idea, the hope of the planetization of life is very much more than a mere matter of biological speculation. It is more of a necessity for our age than the discovery, which we so ardently pursue, of new sources of [physical] energy. It is this idea which can and must bring us the spiritual fire without which all material fires, so laboriously lighted, will presently die down on the surface of the thinking Earth; the fire inspiring us with the joy of action and the zest for life.[9]

CHAPTER 5

Teilhard's Vision and the Earth Charter
Steven C. Rockefeller

I first encountered the work of Pierre Teilhard de Chardin as a divinity student in the classroom of the Christian theologian Daniel Day Williams, at Union Theological Seminary in New York, in the early 1960s. Williams' theology drew heavily on the work of a number of evolutionary thinkers and process philosophers, especially Alfred North Whitehead. Like Whitehead, Teilhard did his most creative work in evolutionary philosophy and theology during the 1920s and 1930s. This was a period that produced a number of highly creative evolutionary philosophers, including Henri Bergson in France, Samuel Alexander in England, and John Dewey in the United States. They were all deeply influenced by science and the experimental method of knowledge, and they all sought in diverse ways—especially Teilhard—to harmonize science, philosophy, and religion in an effort to heal a major split in the modern psyche.

This essay has been prepared as a contribution to "The Spirit of the Earth: Global Ethics and a Sustainable Future," one of a

olid foundation and the process of glob-
on, reversing current dangerous trends.
in world history has generated its own
spiritual consciousness. The quest for a
of the search for our spiritual center as
lobalizing technological civilization.

arter Drafting Process (1992–2000)

Earth Charter.[7] It is a product of the global
began with the drafting of the Charter of
nd the Universal Declaration of Human
s ago. On recommendation of the World
ronment and Development, the 1992 Rio
vored to draft an intergovernmental Earth
et forth fundamental values and principles
ustainable development. As a result of dis-
he North and the South, governments were
Earth Charter. Consequently, in 1994, a new
ive was launched as a civil society undertak-
ng from the Dutch government. The Earth
, which is co-chaired by Maurice Strong and
and made up of members from twenty-one
ng Africa, the Middle East, Asia and the Pa-
he Americas, launched, six years later, the
Peace Palace in The Hague.
ter is a declaration of fundamental principles
ustainable, and peaceful global community. It
ree reasons: the process that produced it, the
ment, and the movement it has inspired. First,
document involved the most open and partici-
t has ever been conducted in connection with
international declaration. It is the product of
rldwide, cross-cultural, interfaith dialogue on

number of panels and events organized as part of a special com-
memoration of the life and thought of Teilhard. It focuses on the
Earth Charter as an articulation of the emerging new global ethics
and as a contribution to what Teilhard called "the formation of a
veritable spirit of the earth."[1]

1. Teilhard and the Spirit of the Earth

Teilhard views the evolution of life on Earth as continuous with
the great evolutionary process that is the universe. Convinced that
all evolution is an ascent toward consciousness, he regards the
emergence of mind in humanity as a great step forward in the
evolutionary process. Teilhard asserts that "the awakening of
thought" and its development "affects life itself in its organic totality and consequently it marks a transformation affecting the
state of the entire planet." In and through the process he labeled
planetization, or what we today call globalization, the cultures and
civilizations, created by the human mind, form above the biosphere a new layer that encircles the planet. Employing the Greek
word for "mind"—*nous*—Teilhard calls this new "thinking envelope" the noosphere. With the development of the mind and noosphere, Teilhard argues that Earth becomes "the thinking earth,"
evolution becomes conscious of itself, and "the spirit of the earth"
begins to take form.[2]

To understand fully Teilhard's meaning it is important to recognize that he views mind as more than simply the power of dis-
cursive reason and scientific knowledge. Mind, he argues, includes
something akin to Plato's *eros*, a passionate longing for the re-
union of the separated and for the good, the true, and the beauti-
ful. One can also say that for Teilhard the mind includes what in
the Bible is called the heart. As a Christian mystic as well as an
experimental scientist, Teilhard argues that God, the center of the

universe, is at work in the world and the entire cosmic evolutionary process is driven by some elemental force seeking to bring the power of mind and love to self-awareness. Furthermore, Teilhard believes that as the noosphere takes form, the evolutionary process will achieve its deeper purpose only insofar as humanity, inspired by God and guided by both love and knowledge, succeeds in unifying the world and building, in the midst of cultural diversity, a just and peaceful planetary civilization.[3]

Teilhard defines love as "the internal propensity to unite" and states that "Love alone is capable of uniting living beings in such a way as to complete and fulfill them; for it alone takes them and joins them by what is deepest in themselves." He envisions humanity's "power of loving developing until it embraces the total of man and of the earth." It is noteworthy that even though Teilhard's work was completed before the environmental movement emerged, in this statement love extends to the whole Earth community—to both people and ecosystems. This is what Teilhard has in mind when he writes of "the spiritual renovation of the earth." Since all elements in the universe are interconnected and interdependent, he rejects as "false and against nature" the idea that human beings who are apart from nature can achieve security and prosperity or that some one fortified society of privileged people can find fulfillment in isolation. "The gates of the future" he argues, "will open only to an advance of all together. . . ." "The Age of Nations is past," he writes. "The task before us now, if we would not perish, is to shake off our ancient prejudices and to build the Earth."[4]

As Teilhard's comments on love suggest, ethical values have a critical role to play in the evolutionary advance of civilization. In addition, from the perspective of his vision of the unification of the world, the formation of global ethics—that is, the emergence of values and principles that are widely shared in all cultures—is a necessary development. The creation of the Earth Charter, which is designed as "an ethical foundation for the emerging

w
th

give international law a s
alization positive directi
Every great civilization
distinctive ethical and s
planetary ethics is part
planetary citizens of a g

Befo
like t
ics in
by itse
the go
ethical
quality
scope o
consequ
cannot d
the huma

Secon
interdepe
powerful,
and social
being of its
among nati
tion, humai
has arrived a
ment where
community i
evolutionary
necessity.[6] Ad
nity requires i
goals and share
ing a further e
sciousness. It ir
on a core of fu

3. *The Earth Ch*

This brings me to the
ethics movement that
the United Nations a
Rights over fifty year
Commission on Envi
Earth Summit endea
Charter that would s
for the transition to
agreements between
not able to draft the I
Earth Charter initia
ing with initial fundi
Charter Commissio
Mikhail Gorbachev
countries representi
cific, Europe and
Earth Charter at th
The Earth Char
for building a just,
is significant for th
content of the doc
the drafting of the
patory process tha
the creation of ar
a decade-long, w

common goals and shared values. Hundreds of organizations and thousands of individuals were engaged in the process. An Earth Charter secretariat was established in Costa Rica at the Earth Council. National Earth Charter committees were set up in fifty different nations. Both grassroots community leaders, including indigenous peoples, and experts in many fields were involved. Meetings were held throughout the world and on the internet. For example, one five-day conference in the Pantanal in Brazil brought together Earth Charter groups from twenty-four countries in South, Central, and North America and the Caribbean and concluded with an outdoor ceremony in celebration of the Earth Charter vision involving local political leaders, a military band, and over 3,000 school children, all wearing Carta da Terra T-shirts.

Second, the content of the Earth Charter reflects the consensus on shared values taking form in the emerging global civil society. The text builds on and extends international law in the fields of environmental conservation and sustainable development. It reflects the findings of the seven UN summit meetings held during the 1990s, especially the summits on environment, population, and women. It reflects a careful study of the ethical visions in over 200 people's treaties and NGO declarations issued over the past three decades and the influence of contemporary thought in science, religion, philosophy, and ethics. The drafting of the Earth Charter was completed several months before the UN Millennium Summit meeting, but its principles fully support the UN Millennium Development Goals. Moreover, the Millennium Development Goals, which may have been influenced by the Earth Charter, can be viewed as steps toward the implementation of Earth Charter principles.

In Teilhard's understanding, as the cosmic evolutionary process unfolds on Earth, it reveals "a fundamental drift towards ever more organized states" that involve increasing physical complexity and psychical interiorization. Teilhard describes this process as "an organico-psychic convergence of the world upon itself,"

culminating in "the reflective interaction of free agents" and a
movement toward social unification globally. From this perspective, the Earth Charter drafting process can be understood as a
response of faith and hope on the part of people in diverse cultures to what Teilhard calls "the forces of unification" at work in
the process of cosmogenesis. Teilhard writes that "the future of
the world . . . is tied up with some sort of social unification of
man—which itself ultimately depends on the free play in our
hearts of certain forces that draw us toward fuller being" involving unity in the midst of complexity and diversity.[8]

4. The Content of the Earth Charter

In and through the intense and often complex debates that occurred during the consultation and drafting process, the organizational structures and wording of the Earth Charter gradually took
form. The Preamble affirms that "Humanity is part of a vast evolving universe" and sets the Charter's ethical principles in the context of a spiritual vision that emphasizes being more, not just
having more. At the heart of the Earth Charter lies an ethic of
respect and care for the community of life as a whole in all its
biological and cultural diversity. Its principles are introduced as
"principles for a sustainable way of life," and they provide an inclusive and integrated understanding of the meaning of sustainable development. Sustainability has emerged as a new guiding
ecological, economic, and social ideal reflecting a deepening realization that the goals of environmental protection, poverty eradication, human rights, gender equality, economic development,
democracy, and peace are all interrelated and interdependent.[9]
   The Earth Charter challenges us to recognize that we are all
citizens of a shared planet as well as citizens of local communities.
Consistent with this view, the Earth Charter expands the ethical
vision dominant in modern industrial technological society in a
three-fold fashion. First, it seeks to deepen commitment to the

human rights and human development of all the world's peoples, especially the poor, the vulnerable, and oppressed. In this regard, it promotes gender equality, economic equity, the eradication of poverty, and participatory, transparent, and accountable democratic governance at all levels. Second, its goal is to awaken a new commitment to the human rights and well-being of future generations. Intergenerational responsibility, holistic thinking, and long-term planning are core values of the ethics of sustainable living. Third, its goal is to promote recognition that all life forms are interdependent members of the one community of life on Earth and all are worthy of respect and moral consideration.

There are two reasons to respect the larger living world. The first is the anthropocentric reason cited in the UN Millennium Declaration.[10] We are dependent on the goods and services provided by Earth's ecosystems. It is, therefore, in our self-interest to protect and restore ecosystems and their biodiversity. Second, as affirmed by the World Charter for Nature (1982) and the Convention on Biological Diversity (1992), all life forms have value regardless of their utilitarian value to people. In other words, they possess what some philosophers call intrinsic value. It is for this reason that the greater community of life and each life form is worthy of moral consideration. As the 1987 report of the World Commission on Environment and Development, *Our Common Future*, puts it: "the case for the conservation of nature should not rest only with development goals. It is part of our moral obligation to other living beings and future generations."[11] It is quite probable that unless societies come to respect nature for itself as well as for its utilitarian value to people, it will not be possible to generate the change in human behavior necessary to achieve sustainability.

The Earth Charter is often described as a declaration of global interdependence and universal responsibility; it adopted the concept of universal responsibility in part because it complements the idea of universal human rights. We all have rights, and with those

rights we have responsibilities. Our ecological and social responsibilities, of course, are common but differentiated depending on
our situations and capacities. In addition, since we live in a world
where everything is interconnected, each one of us is to one degree or another responsible to all other beings for how we live
and act. In this sense, too, our responsibility is universal. This
idea is expressed clearly in the Preamble of the Earth Charter,
which states that if we are to build a sustainable world community, "it is imperative that we, the peoples of Earth, declare our
responsibility to one another, to the greater community of life,
and to future generations." Reflecting the influence of the Earth
Charter, the Johannesburg Declaration issued by the World Summit on Sustainable Development in 2002 contains an identical
affirmation of universal responsibility.[12]

Teilhard asserts that "the evolution of responsibility is simply
one particular aspect of cosmogenesis." It is an expression on the
level of human consciousness of the interdependence that is a fundamental characteristic of all things throughout the universe. He
explains that the scope of human responsibility and solidarity expands to embrace all humanity and the whole Earth community
as the interconnections among peoples intensify under the impact
of population increases, new technologies, and globalization. The
energy of love and the sense of universal responsibility grow with
what Teilhard calls "the Sense of Earth," by which he means "the
passionate sense of common destiny." He states that "the only
truly natural and real human Unity is the Spirit of Earth." In
addition, he emphasizes that, given its cosmic roots, the sense of
responsibility and the "new ethics of the Earth" are not merely
social conventions that we can ignore if we choose but "organic
bonds" that we neglect at our peril.[13]

The Earth Charter principles provide government, business,
and civil society with a clear vision of the revolutionary changes
needed if humanity is to achieve a sustainable way of living. As
the Preamble indicates, the document is intended to serve as "a

common standard by which the conduct of all individuals, organizations, businesses, governments, and transnational institutions is
to be guided and assessed." However, the Earth Charter limits
itself to broad ethical principles and general guidelines and does
not attempt to identify the specific mechanisms and regulations
that societies must adopt to implement its principles. Different
cultures and societies will, of course, find many diverse ways of
achieving the goal of sustainability.

The Earth Charter principles culminate with a vision of a culture of tolerance, nonviolence, and peace. The peace principle
comes last—in Principle 16—because building a culture of peace
requires implementation of all the other principles. Peace is described as "the wholeness created by right relationship with oneself, other persons, other cultures, other life, Earth, and the larger
whole of which all are a part." (16f) So defined, peace is conceived
as an inclusive ethical and spiritual value consistent with Teilhard's concept of "the Spirit of Earth."

5. The Earth Charter Movement

There is a third reason the Earth Charter is proving to be a significant document. An Earth Charter movement has emerged as
part of the larger international sustainable development movement. Since the Earth Charter was formally launched in June
2000, it has been translated into thirty languages and dissemin-
ated around the world by the Earth Charter secretariat, which is
affiliated with the UN University for Peace in Costa Rica. The
document has been endorsed by thousands of NGOs and by several hundred individual cities as well as the International Council
of Local Environmental Initiatives (ICLEI) and the US Conference of Mayors. Last November IUCN (The World Conservation Union), which is the largest and most influential international
conservation organization, including among its members seventy-
seven state governments and over 800 NGOs, endorsed the Earth

Charter at its World Conservation Congress in Bangkok and recognized the Earth Charter as an ethical guide for IUCN policy.

Global Community Initiatives and The World Resources Institute have designed a new guidebook and computer software
program entitled the Earth Charter Community Action Tool or
EarthCAT to assist local governments with developing goals,
strategies, and measurable indicators for the implementation of
Earth Charter principles.[14] These materials will be translated and
tested in cities in Canada, Jordan, Peru, Senegal, South Africa,
the Ukraine, the US and possibly China. For example, the City
of Calgary in Alberta, Canada, is using the Earth Charter and
EarthCAT in its effort to create a 100-year plan for the city.

The Earth Charter is also being widely used in schools, univer-
sities, and faith communities as a vehicle for exploring the critical
choices before humanity and the meaning of global ethics and
sustainable development. The UNESCO General Conference of
member states endorsed the Earth Charter in 2003 as "an important ethical framework for sustainable development" and as "an
educational tool." UNESCO is collaborating with the Earth
Charter Initiative as materials are being prepared for the UN
Decade of Education for Sustainable Development (DESD) that
was launched at the United Nations headquarters on March 1st,
2005.[15] In the spirit of the decade, the national Ministry of Education in Costa Rica is already distributing a teachers' guide on
"Education for Sustainable Development with the Earth Charter" and related materials for students. Teilhard, who believed
that the Roman Catholic Church and other religious organizations had a critical role to play in promoting a transformation of
human consciousness, and who recognized the vital importance
of science and education organizations and the United Nations,
would undoubtedly have enthusiastically supported the DESD
and its goals.

In conclusion, the Earth Charter provides a much-needed integrated vision of the way forward in the form of broad ethical
guidelines. Its emphasis on a transformation of our ethical values

reflects a recognition that even though UN summit meetings and international conferences have developed a promising vision of a better world for all, the political will is too often lacking because the ethical commitment is at best half-hearted. The Earth Charter is one expression of what Teilhard calls "the Spirit of Earth" that is struggling to come to full consciousness in all of us. It is a vision of the ideal, but the ideals in the Earth Charter are real possibilities. We have the knowledge and technological expertise to progressively implement the Charter's principles while maintaining a vibrant economy. Even though the challenges before us are daunting and there are powerful forces of resistance, progress is being made on many fronts, and much more can be done. The spirit of change is in the air. Teilhard de Chardin's writings express great hope regarding the future. His hope springs from a religious faith that includes a profound sense of belonging to the unfolding universe, faith in the human potential, and a mystical intuition that love and unity are the deeper meaning of the evolutionary and historical processes. Teilhard assures us that if we have the wisdom and courage to embrace a vision for the future informed both by the head and the heart, science and faith, we will find our way.

Teilhard and Economic Globalization

Teilhard, Globalization, and the Future of Humanity

Michel Camdessus

Globalization and the future of humanity: The second of these terms is Teilhardian; the first is not. Between these two there is an initiative to be brought forth, and the United Nations Organization is at the heart of the system that humanity has made to accomplish this task. It is as a man of this system that I wish to engage in this reflection, but I would like to first share some passages from Teilhard de Chardin that have, I dare say, accompanied me and directed me on my path of maturation. Then I will offer my own understanding of globalization, and we will thus be able to discern how we might proceed in a Teilhardian light—that is to say, from a more mastered globalization process toward the future of humanity.

1. Teilhard de Chardin: A Leap

How are we to unify our lives, bringing together faith and action? What will be the results of our actions? Will those results pass with time or will they contribute to the accomplishment of creation, to its restoration in a new, long-awaited and hoped for Earth? These were my questions, as well as those of my generation. Teilhard, in answering them, revealed to us an image of Christian perfection of the human effort. In rereading the words below, I understand better how their lyricism and fervor touched me so profoundly.

> In virtue of a wonderfully augmenting strength included in things, every reality that is reached and surpassed brings us both to the discovery and the search of an ideal of superior spiritual quality. For he who adequately casts his sail to the wind of the earth, a current is made manifest that forces him towards the high seas. The more a man desires and thus acts nobly, the more he becomes avidly interested in pursuing large and sublime objects. The only family, the only country, the only re-numerating face of his action is no longer sufficient. He will need to create general organizations, mark out new paths, sustain new causes, discover new truths, and nourish and defend a new ideal. As a result, little by little, the earth's laborer no longer belongs to himself. Little by little, the great wind of the universe, insinuated in him by the fissure of a humble but faithful action, has expanded, elevated, and carried him. For the Christian, assuming he knows how to make use of the resources of his faith, these effects attain their paroxysm and culmination. . . . He will need to create general organizations.[1]

Following are his writings on the divinization of actions and passivities. It's the first, actions, rather than the second that fascinates one at twenty years of age, though the divinization of all passivities is just as important a concept. "Passivities" has to do with all those forms of subjection and diminution that assail us, and that without pause "painfully interfere with our tendencies, that broach or reroute our journey towards the *plus-être*, [and] that reduce our real or apparent developmental capacities."[2] We know well that the more we seek to expand our action to a more ample, and especially universal, horizon, the more we encounter such passivities. In a life of faith, these passivities can, and indeed are, converted into positive and precious contributions leading to the fulfillment of creation. But when we are twenty years old, passivities are not what seize us, for amongst the three categories of human beings presented in Teilhard's "Reflections on Happiness" (the tired, the joyous, and the ardent), it's the option of the ardent that we choose:

> Those for whom to live is an ascension, a discovery. We can humor these men, treat them as being naïve, or find them bothersome. But in the meantime it is they who made us, and it is from them that the Earth of tomorrow will come.[3]

Teilhard did not influence me through his prestigious work as a scientist, for it was outside my area of study; rather, it was his faith in God, in humanity, and the world that touched me. His words were in symphonic accord with those of Mounier and Perroux, inviting engagement and interior freedom—engagement because we are not responsible for ourselves without being responsible for others and the world. But Teilhard's message went further than that of the personalist philosophers such as Mounier, because he is first and foremost a master of the spiritual life. With him, "all is sacred"; he enjoins us to "understand and measure the power of divinization contained in a love of neighbor" conceived in the largest sense. At the heart of his message there lies the unifying action of love that supernaturalizes all action. If one has received such a word, how can he not try to make of his life an effort to make the world a better place to live, and bring humankind closer together in greater solidarity through a joint effort involving all humans, in all the diversity of actions that compete to humanize the world, in intimate complicity with the unifying work of the Spirit?

In short, when we cross the threshold from the personal into the professional world, we receive a new sort of confirmation in the faith as well as a new hope of a Christ unimaginably greater than the one presented to us in all the available catechisms. It is a Christ who makes himself one with the Earth. The genius of Teilhard was to discover for the twentieth century the vivid intuition of St. Paul at the dawn of Christianity. This reveals both the total and totalizing Christ, the one who "will sum up under himself the entire Universe, what is in heaven and on earth,"[4] as well as "creation, delivered to the power of death . . . but which nonetheless has kept the hope of being liberated from bondage, from inevitable degradation so as to know the liberty and the glory of the children of God."[5] For Teilhard, in line with St. Paul, Christ is "the omega in whom is brought, at the expansive cone's summit, all daughters, sons, and generations of the Universe."[6] He is the omega who is both divine Person and place of hyperpersonalizing convergence for evolution and the long labors of men. He is the ultimate "amorizing" point of history who mysteriously attracts all toward himself. "Christ, Center of the Universe, reuniting all things and returning them on the last day to his Father so that God might be all in all."[7] Those words are the last ones he wrote—fifty years ago, on the 7th of April, 1955—on the last page of his journal.

It is a Christ engaged once for all in the history of men, in the future of humanity, in solidarity with us above all our own efforts to understand (at whatever level they might be) for the success of history; a success of history which can be nothing other than an "amorization," and thus divinization, of the world. From here there is also the revelation of a charity of another sort. Charity is the amorizing action in a life of service to men directed toward a participation in the construction and organization of a world that is more livable. It is also a construction of "this new Earth" which God will pull from the efforts of men spanning the breadth of history: What wonderful dignity belongs then to this work where God and humanity join hands to make of our history a sacred history. Teilhard states it more forcefully: "The reign of Christ, to which we have vowed ourselves, can only establish itself to the extremes of its humanization . . . on an Earth supported by all the voices of the technical arts and the intellectual sciences."[8]

The extreme of its humanization! What a precious message for a generation that has had to situate itself before the phenomenon of globalization, of which Teilhard de Chardin had already seen the first indications, and which were followed by a prodigious acceleration. From the beginning this phenomenon was fascinating to the disciples of Teilhard. Did it not appear as a movement advancing with giant steps toward the unity of the world? Wasn't it the phenomenon that Teilhard had a premonition of as being like a step in this "Universal unification process through which God himself attracts men," and that he encouraged us to accept in "great common hope" . . . a passionate taste of development and being?

To make sense of globalization, Teilhard gave us several insights to guide our thinking about it, as well as several rare but powerful ways of how we might act on it, and transform it into a disciplined future for humanity. It is important to try to discern the threats and prospects of globalization before situating it as the future of humanity.

2. *Globalization: Threats and Opportunities*

Let us first try to accurately discern the opportunities and threats of globalization, not an easy task as the world, carried onward by its acceleration, seems to be more out of control with each day. Jean-Baptiste de Foucauld says it well: "The more the world becomes globalized, the more the global escapes our grasp, the less it can be mastered."[9] Although this analysis is hardly in line with Teilhard's vision, it is certainly respectable, and it is the conclusion, based on a geopolitical analysis, of Jean-Luc Domenach, in which he observes how our world conforms so little to Teilhard's vision.[10] The speed with which changes are made in the globalized world is observed by public opinion, which feeds its fears and doubts.

Read from the standpoint of the economist it is clear that globalization is a unique mix of risks and opportunities. The risks are evident, but they can't allow us to neglect the opportunities globalization entails, if only because they will all have to be put to use if we want to confront all the risks. Let us measure these risks. They are multiple and often justly noted. I'd like to highlight four of them:

1. Financial instability.

2. Inability of the nation-state to deal with new problems that manifest themselves on a global scale.

3. Cultural annihilation.

4. The "ultimate systematic challenge"—the blatantly evident inequalities and the marginalization of the poor.

The first of these risks is financial insecurity. In the recent past, several costly crises have shaken the global economy. The pronounced turbulence in currency exchanges, the crisis in emerging markets triggered by the events in Mexico that then spread to Asia and Russia and back again to Latin America, the collapse of several large financial institutions, and the scandals of ENRON and WorldCom, all indicate the weaknesses of our system. We now know that a financial crisis can start almost anywhere in the world and spread like a trail of gunpowder, resulting in the increased misery of those who are most vulnerable. The Asian crisis of the nineties taught us this very lesson. We are now living in a much greater state of interdependence than we had imagined possible. All it takes is one country to collapse, even one of a modest size like Thailand, and the whole world economy is in jeopardy. All of these crises have created millions of victims of poverty and unemployment. We have tried to contain them, but much still needs to be done to truly stabilize and civilize the global financial system.

The second risk constitutes, in itself, what are in fact the developments of the twenty-first century: the continual welling up of problems (climate change, financial crime, drugs, information piracy, migration, large epidemics, and others) that ignore the boundaries of nation-states, and in the face of which these states are powerless. It is now as if a split is being established between the globalization of productive systems, between the thousands of variables affecting our lives on one side, and on the other side the slow pace of progress of the political bodies who should be responding to these new questions. The proliferating uncertainties might prompt our contemporaries to pose the question: "Is there a pilot on our plane as we make our way through the heart of this ever-increasing turbulence?"

A third risk affects human societies at their very heart: their cultural identity. A Babel-like unification of the world, and the crushing of the treasure which is the diversity of these cultures, represents the opposite of the personalizing unification of the world. As this risk reverses the opportunities that globalization presents to the cultural enrichment of the world, reaction is indispensable.

The heterogeneity of the globalizing process, in conjunction with the inequality of its benefits, creates another risk—that of the marginalization of countries and whole regions. The case of Africa is the most tragic, and one that raises many questions. While some developing countries have understood how to seize the forces of globalization so as to accelerate their pace toward economic progress, not all have. Those countries incapable of participating in the expansion of global commerce, or of attracting a sizable volume of private investment, risk being forgotten in the market of the global economy. The countries most exposed to this risk are precisely those poor countries that are desperately in need of markets, investments, and the growth that globalization could bring them. Everything has happened as if the poorest countries have no place on the map of global investments, and

there is reason to fear that the gulf is still widening between rich
and poor countries.

At times the world has even seemed to resign itself to this reality, as if we could settle for cutting short our losses. But since
September 11th we know better. Neither violence, nor misery,
is confined; these evils are systemic, like contagious diseases and
environmental degradation. In this era of globalization there is no
longer room for the old illusion of a prosperity hidden behind the
walls of a fortified Western world. Though it is Africa that has all
the symptoms of absolute poverty, this evil affects us all and we
will only rid ourselves of it by working together. If we do not find
better means to create opportunities for the poor, the situation
will worsen, and become more of a threat in tandem with the
demographic clock that continues to tick. According to studies,
there will be two billion more people alive in twenty-five years
than there are today, of which more than ninety percent will be
born in developing countries. Many spiritual leaders have reminded us of this reality, and Pope John Paul II has articulated
the situation in such clear terms, in his encyclical "Solicitudo rei
Socialis:" "Development either becomes shared in common by
every part of the world or it undergoes a process of regression
even in zones marked by constant progress."[11] Development must
therefore be a common process, but for this to happen we need
to know how to seize the opportunities globalization offers us in
order to build a better future.

These opportunities, at closer look, are rather impressive.
Since the seventies, the exchange in goods and services between
countries and continents has nearly tripled. The increase in foreign direct investment (FDI) has seen remarkable growth as well,
and is now in excess of 800 billion dollars a year. The level of
integration in financial markets today is without historical precedent. The combined influence of economic market expansion,
global unification of currency markets, and the boom in new information and communication technologies has created objec-
tively favorable conditions for the development of the world

economy. Teilhard, who was so enthused by the first cyclotron, would have welcomed with great ardor the advent of the internet and the creation of a universal information-based economy. These opportunities hold out the hope of accelerating development, and creating the necessary conditions for the Southern Hemispheric countries that are ready to join the integrative current of the world economy. Have we not helped millions of people quickly enter into the global economy who but a few short years ago were still on the fringes? It is certainly a prodigious and fundamentally positive development in human history. These new arrivals are principally the poor laborers of large, emerging countries, and they legitimately aspire to greater prosperity and wealth. Let us therefore see what globalization is first and foremost: a fantastic moment of progress in which countless numbers of Chinese, Indians, and others are pulling themselves away from their conditions of extreme misery.

Let us add to this the quantity of exponential advances that have been accelerated by the network of think-tanks and by scientific progress. If Teilhard had witnessed these, he would have been jubilant. Certainly, there are risks with regard to the manipulation of the human being, but there are also innumerable opportunities: the decryption of the mysteries of the living being, an economy that is more respectful of the environment, and the advancement of information and communication technologies.

All told, we can see in the forces of globalization a set of dynamics working at the service of man's brightest qualities: his creativity, his sense of solidarity, and his sense of responsibility for the world in its totality. With such a set of dynamics we are in a world which is not without disorder, many troubles and much suffering, but is improving because of the accruing speed of the spread of knowledge, the greater opportunities for travel and establishing contacts, and the responsiveness of societies to the woes suffered by peoples at the furthest extremities of the globe, as seen, for example, in the recent tsunami. We are evermore aware of the fact that the world is becoming more closely knit. All major

events, even tragic ones, nourish this growing universal perception of globalization, and lend greater viability to the opportunity
of bringing about a universal civil society, one already found at
the origin of many of mankind's achievements in the twentieth
century. In one word, they are opportunities.

Threats and opportunities! But let us recognize, for the sake of
our European contemporaries, that the threats seem to outweigh
the hope of defeating our atavistic woes. Many have given up
hope, basing their hopelessness on an old premise that multinational organizations have an unquenchable thirst for power, while
others still dream of the day when there will be a universal popular uprising overthrowing the system. This is, however, another
way of losing oneself in illusions. Our world, in its complexity
and confusion, is once again at the cusp of a "critical moment."
Everything is happening as if the decades in which we live now,
that appear to belong to the era envisioned by Teilhard (that is
to say, the "planetization" of our society), are not fulfilling their
potential. "Planetization," according to Teilhard, takes place in
the dual process of convergence and personalization. As it is, one
of the two has taken longer to manifest itself. Personalization has
been detached from convergence, and the fulcrum of our crisis is
to be found here. Recall that Teilhard had forewarned us about
this "critical point." He wrote the following to his friend, Abbé
Gaudefroy, in February 1935:

> It seems to me psychologically inevitable that, in the next two
> or three generations, Humanity will ask itself what is the meaning
> and value of the pain it inflicts on itself; and I have little doubt
> that the answer will be an act of faith in the Future. Otherwise it
> would be the end of Evolution. I think, as you do, that we are on
> the cusp of a critical moment. . . .[12]

Two or three generations—here we are! What should we do? The
answer is easy to formulate: The task given is to carry forward the
progress of personalization, on the material plane, to rapidly bind

the world together more tightly. This is how we are to move forward from this "critical point" toward the future of humanity; we are to humanize this world of ours, which is our "divine milieu."

3. From the "Critical Moment"—Today— to the Future of Humanity

Although he never pretended to be knowledgeable in public policy or in economic and social matters, Teilhard de Chardin left to those who would, in the future, be in charge of world affairs, several points of orientation so that their efforts might be directed toward "a humanizing perspective." These orientations are reducible to three essential recommendations:

- "Act together, in a grand and common hope."
- Build world cohesion.
- Promote human solidarity.

Each of these three orientations calls for some commentary. "Act together"—first and foremost an act of significant mutual confidence!—"in a grand, common hope." I can't help but think, as relates to this point, about the institution that I directed for thirteen years. Part of my responsibility was to "give confidence to all its members." This included convincing problem-wracked countries that they could overcome their difficulties, that there was never a hopeless case in human affairs, that if they deployed all their efforts the international response would not be lacking. Then I would seek to garner support for these countries (of which the world had despaired) from enough of their friends so as to allow them to retake their place in the community of nations. It was surely a difficult, but indeed fascinating, task.

We should identify the orientations that might occur beyond this common confidence and hope, to draw together more closely the principles of convergence and personalization, cohesion and solidarity. Multilateralism is clearly, ever since the Second World War, the first of these, which was developed in response to the attitude of "every nation for itself" that had instigated the war, and which seems to remain today the response to problems of universal dimensions. Although its progress can appear despairingly slow, and we may even go through periods when unilateralism seems to hold the advantage, it remains the unquestionable approach. Multilateralism, in effect, offers the opportunity to all countries, from the largest to the smallest, to assume their responsibility in solving the universal problems that can only be efficiently broached at the global level. This explains the importance of the project undertaken today to revamp the structures intended to serve the common universal good. The effort to reform the United Nations, as well as global financial institutions, should enhance this process and intensify the process of reflection concerning global public goods.

In fact, what is needed is for the system inherited from the postwar era to be replaced by a system reformed in a spirit of subsidiarity that responds to the problems brought to the fore by globalization. This new system also needs to put in place a framework of global regulations designed to deal with global problems. This reform, like that of financial institutions, will take form only if the means are found to give a rightful place to poor countries in instances of decision making. That is why I find the initiative to expand the G7 by opening it up to representatives of the third world, forming a sort of Economic and Social Security Council, so important. The emergence of this governance body would be but a first step. We have to work toward what John XXIII, that other prophet, sought forty years ago—not a world government, but a "public authority of universal competence" in those areas where it is needed.

For such a change to be possible on a global level, it is equally necessary that Europe fully exercise, without timidity, a partnership role with the United States. Europe had the historic chance of successfully experiencing the creation of amicable integrative structures in an environment where there had been nothing but secular suspicion and hatred. Now it must also show itself ready and willing to assume sole leadership for the common good in those instances where the United States recuses itself. Such an approach toward partnership for the common good could have historic importance, and it could also chart a new course for diplomacy by rejecting a longstanding view that envisioned relations between states as being dehumanized and cold. As Europeans, we are citizens of the world's premier commercial body, and therefore we must be conscious of the dimensions of both our citizenship and our responsibility: national, European, and global; in assuming them as we ought, we will be better able to participate in the immense global effort to humanize the world.

Besides the advantages multilateralism engenders for better world governance, partnership presents another means to progress. Adopted as a central strategy for North-South relations during the Monterey conference of 2001, it aims to replace the system of assistance-based relations, of which we have all come to identify the inadequacies, with a system of relations whereby all countries pursue a common responsibility for the success of all. All recognize that the significant problems of the world, starting with extreme poverty, are everyone's problems, and that they must be dealt with by all people working together. Herein lies a significant transformation, for partnership implies dialogue between equals. It implies that your partner in dialogue defines, by his own initiative, his own choices and priorities. It also implies frankness on both sides, as well as your acceptance of the other's scrutinizing of that dimension of your activity that relates to him. It implies a profound respect of the other's ethical exigencies, his culture, and his traditions, in all situations, including that of the organization of collective living. It implies that no party defaults on its responsibility to the other. Finally, it implies the acceptance of a common journey on the new path of globalization, along with all that this entails with respect to the other's progress.

A particular application of this approach is being initiated in the NEPAD (New Economic Partnership for African Development) framework between the G8 and Africa. It comprises, for the first time in history, an offer of partnership that the African countries made to the G8 in 2001 at Genoa, and that the G8 countries accepted. The Commission for Africa, launched and presided over by Prime Minister Tony Blair, has just repeated that herein lies the most certain path toward decisive African progress.

Partnership must no longer remain a state-to-state project. Rather, it must be multidimensional. It ought to extend to enterprises, financial institutions, and civil society. We are far too accustomed to leaving responsibility for drawing up initiatives on matters of international life to states. Let us not pass quick judgment on those large enterprises that are trying to respond to Kofi Annan's request for such partnerships. Many of them have an authentic recognition of the solidarity they share in the development of the countries where they work. But allow me to emphasize most particularly the role of civil society. It can have a major role in the construction of the future through constant personalizing action. The future of the world is in its hands. Convergence and personalization can only proceed together if this concern is fully addressed by a civil society to which we all belong—a civil society that needs to be better organized to be able to monitor what we are doing in its name.

In English there is the expression: "Act locally, think globally." The "act locally" is not the shrinking of a gloriously universal action. Rather, it's the opposite: It's an essential action. It is put to work in the manner that the authors of the Universal Declaration on Human Rights recognized as binding to all men: Act in all things "in a spirit of fraternity." All action carried out in a fraternal spirit, no matter how modest, helps to build civilization. For Christians it is an essential component of what they seek to build, namely the "civilization of love" that John Paul II untiringly called for.

In this construction of cohesive and global solidarity we cannot ignore the essential dimension of respect for binding agreements. The world has accustomed itself to organizing large conferences and concluding them with the signing of grand engagements, only to quickly forget these agreements. There is need here for a radical change. We must, as citizens, demand that our commitments be respected, all the more because they were reiterated during the UN conference held in New York in September 2000. During this conference celebrating the new millennium, 170 heads of state reiterated the major agreements made in the course of the nineties, agreements that we have all more or less forgotten.[13]

We must hold to these commitments. The international community has made a good resolution to review every five years where we stand with respect to these commitments. It is what will happen here this coming September, and we have a pretty good sense of what to expect. Even if the results are satisfactory in certain parts of the world, those for Africa will remain very worrisome, and we will thus have to correct our course.

In the past few months I have participated on the work of the Commission for Africa precisely in order to identify what this correction might entail. We have highlighted the significance of the additional cooperation needed between African nations and the industrialized countries: Double the finances, cancel debts when absolutely necessary, and review the nature of our commercial relations. But the Commission especially underlined the fact that no situation is hopeless if the community of humans decides to collectively tackle it in its search for cohesion and solidarity. Africa today is assuming its obligations better than ever, and it is thus the moment to join forces so as to give it the decisive support it needs to have a chance at rejoining the current of global economic integration.

I wish to insist on this obligation to respect commitments. It's the first necessary condition for achieving cohesion, for all of human society rests on commitments. To take this obligation

lightly is to negate all chances of advancing toward a more fraternal society. We know where these methods take us: to the cruel
game of unregulated market forces. Thus, the first step toward
globalizing solidarity is respect for established commitments.

Finally, the concept of sustainable development and the politics that it inspires, especially the promotion of global public
goods, is another indispensable dimension in the construction of
the future. Its structure contains in itself three dimensions that
are profoundly in sync with Teilhard's vision: first, the "world
developments" that he daily consecrated in his "mass on the
world;" second, the demand for a development oriented toward
social cohesion; and last, respect for creation and its fragility, that
no one loved more than he, as it stands in peril of being pillaged.

This concept of sustainable development is now at the heart
of global institutions' politics, and is the origin of many global
organizational efforts. It illustrates well the fecundity of Teilhard's thought, as well as its contribution to the organization of
the world. Just like the multilateralism, partnership, cohesion and
solidarity that I have just evoked, this last concept of sustainable
development will only be able to continue growing if it continues
to be vigorously carried forward, in a spirit of global citizenship,
by civil society. Its emergence on a universal level is, in parallel
and synergistic fashion with the establishment of global institutions, one of the manifestations of what could be the advent of
the noosphere. It's already at the origin of many advances toward
a more just world.

It's in the ranks of civil society that this universal dimension
of citizenship is essential for a new, veritably democratic global
governance structure to develop. As long as non-governmental
organizations are free of political influence, transparent in their
financial affairs, respectful of democratic legitimacy, and uncom-
promising with respect to the truth and non-violence, they can,
in many circumstances, be the avant-garde of this process. NGOs,
like multilateral institutions, must not give up the effort when
faced with the difficulties of the present age. Our friend would

have said: "Let us conjure up the threat of strikes in the noosphere."

Conclusion

Here then are several paths toward humanization and globalization that the international community is trying to open so as to give every person a rightful place. This is a task that many have given themselves to in hope, finding in it their full realization as men and women. It is a modest path, insufficient in many respects and often judged harshly, that is constantly at risk of being doubted or abandoned due to inertia or the pressure of contrary forces. Let us not hide the fact that it is a difficult path where a new effort is needed at every turn, and where we are reminded at every step, that the necessary change must begin with us! Progress is therefore often uncertain, under the assault of critiques—St. John of the Cross would have said: "aunque es de noche" (although it is night). The task's difficulties, even its setbacks, would not have surprised Teilhard de Chardin, or reduced his enthusiasm. He would have recognized such developments to be in line with his intuitions concerning the noosphere: stupefying developments in research and communications, growing awareness of exigencies—both those of solidarity and ecology—and the evidence of a world becoming more tightly knit. He would even recognize the progress made toward "this spirit of fraternity," this duty that none dare now remind us of. It's fraternity that will save the noosphere. Will it bring us to this ultra human that Teilhard was outlining in his last reflections? Father de Lubac said that this is risky extrapolation. Without entering into this debate now, let me say that if Teilhard were to face the fragility of all our efforts, he would probably feel more intensely what he called "the necessity of specifying and organizing the total natural-human effort."[14] In September 2000, before the World Bank and the IMF, President Havel, an agnostic, spoke in the same vein of the need to add a new sort of restructuration to the effort these institutions must promote: "I believe that it is time to think of a new restructuring: that of the value system on which our current civilization rests."[15]

How do we restructure a value system? Without illusion, Havel added: "We will have difficulty in achieving this end if we do not find in our hearts the strength to question and to re-found an order of values that we would be ready to share and honor despite our diversity, and to link these new values with something that is situated beyond the horizon of either immediate interests, or a given person or group. But how can we achieve this goal without a new, powerful influx of human spirituality?"[16] A spiritual leap that, for Teilhard, should realize itself in "a similarly profound aspiration" directed not toward Something, but rather Someone: this someone who has been working from the beginning for the "amorization" of evolution, this someone who "himself attracts men, and reaches them through the unifying process of the Universe."[17] May we all, therefore, my dear friends, in the footsteps of Pierre Teilhard de Chardin, and according to the words of Rilke, hear, in the tumult of our world, "the imperceptible noise that God makes as he divinely exercises his work of love and slowness."[18]

Translated by Mark Doherty, S.J.

CHAPTER 7

Teilhard and Globalization
Jean Boissonnat

The word is recent; the reality is ancient. The use of the word *globalization* in the sense that we mean it today apparently derives from the definition given by an American economist, Theodore Levitt, in an article published in 1983: multiplication of trade, universal competition, and the extension of great industrial networks.

Before we go further in examining this phenomenon, it is helpful to give it some historical context. Globalization as Teilhard understood it includes not only an evolution of economic life, but also evolution itself: as a universal destination that goes well beyond the limits of our planet. The fundamental intuition of Teilhard was that the creation of the world was not finished. It is developing according to certain laws, perhaps not scientifically defined, but still rigorous, of increasing convergence and growing consciousness. The human race holds a strategic place in this development because God manifested himself as Christ, as a human being, not a stone, flower, bird, or elephant. Teilhard wrote in the 1920s: "We imagine perhaps that creation has been finished for a

between organized forces, constitutes an institutionalization of violence in order to give it some order. We "declare war," we "conclude a peace," we "sign treaties." We do this so that eruptions of violence might have a clear beginning and end. Our great historian Pierre Chaunu ascertained what humanity has gained by the transition from original violence to this organized, institutionalized, and regulated violence. Where ten human beings once were killed by other human beings, and not by famine, epidemics, or other natural catastrophes, no more than one perishes in the historic phase of organized violence. Still the toll remains a heavy one: 100 million deaths in the twentieth century due to war and revolutions.

Economic life constitutes along with sports the greatest effort of humanity to lighten the weight of violence by moving it away from human beings toward things. It is organized in a competition where what one wins is not necessarily lost by the other. The market relationship does not attempt to bring about the collapse of one of the two parties through competition; the seller does not want to ruin the buyer because the seller needs the buyer to continue buying. The consumer cannot desire the failure of the producer because the consumer needs the producer for his or her acquisitions. This "win-win" relationship thus becomes natural because it satisfies the needs of both parties. In reality harmony is obviously not guaranteed in every situation. Numerous instances of abuse, exploitation, and injustice exist. Violence remains present in unemployment, financial crashes, and illicit profits. "The economy contains violence," according to the fine phrase of Jean-Pierre Dupuy, in both senses of the expression: it both contains and limits. This is probably why the economy has been the most effective vehicle of the accelerated globalization that we are living through today. This does not mean that globalization only offers an economic dimension. In multiplying the avenues of communication, it touches all the aspects of human life: culture, politics, art, and religion.

2. Major Stages of Globalization

The first great stage of globalization, called "the great discoveries" in the fifteenth and sixteenth centuries, might appear quite modest. The first voyage around the world was completed in 1522, but transoceanic trade remained minimal. Moreover, the largest part of the world's population ignored these geographical discoveries. Despite the alphabet, writing, and printing, nine-tenths of the population in Europe did not know how to read at the end of the Renaissance. Their geographic horizon was limited to a circle of five kilometers. The surplus of wealth created by this opening on the world has been estimated to be approximately 1% of the period's production.[2] Nonetheless, the seventeenth century combines this modest gain in economic capital with an extraordinary coefficient of intellectual capital with the conceptual revolutions of Kepler, Galileo, Descartes, Leibniz, and Newton. In less than fifty years humanity learned to describe the world in mathematical terms.

This was the first great economic revolution since the transition to agriculture ten thousand years earlier, which led to the industrial revolution at the end of the eighteenth century. It took time for all these intellectual and technological achievements to have their effect and to bear fruit, and for the managers of society to authorize their functioning.

Mentality has changed since the end of the Middle Ages. People no longer expect that the economy will assure the survival of the species by satisfying its natural needs for food, clothing, and shelter. Superimposed over this economy of subsistence, which has dominated humanity from its origins, is an economy of development, in which needs are no longer defined by nature, but by culture, because the true nature of humanity is its culture. These are the "social" needs that are transmitted and thus expanded through a mimetic process. The satisfaction of one of these needs quickly produces the appearance of new needs. This unceasing expansion remains the purpose of our economy and explains our

fascination with the concept of growth and our incessant calculation of the evolution and comparison of "per capita income."

According to the estimates of Angus Maddison, the growth of
productivity was stagnant during the first millennium of the
Christian era.[3] Since population itself was stagnant (with strong
oscillations caused by famines, wars, epidemics, natural disasters)
and situated around 250 million people (already mainly in Asia),
the result was that per capita income remained unchanged. During the first eight centuries of the second millennium of the
Christian era, economic growth rose (+0.22% per annum), but
the population also rose, reaching a billion human beings by the
beginning of the nineteenth century. The result was that the per
capita income only showed weak growth (+0.05% per annum),
albeit with clear differences according to the continents and the
social classes. The momentum had arrived. Humanity discovered
economic growth, the fruit of work productivity. In the course of
the last two hundred years, world production has increased by
2.21% annually. Despite an unprecedented population explosion
(the population grew from one to six billion people), per capita
income has risen by 1.21% per annum. Obviously these revenues
are marked by strong disparities. Whereas per capita income was
roughly equal everywhere during the first millennium of the
Christian era (approximately twelve times less than the current
world average), today it is twenty times more elevated in North
America than in Africa.

The growth of per capita revenue literally took off during the
second part of the twentieth century: from 1950 to 1973, +4.08%
per annum in Western Europe (catching up on the losses related
to the last war), +8.05% in Japan. The rhythm of growth became
approximately 1 to 3% in Europe, America, and Japan during the
last quarter of the century, while it took off in Asia (especially
China) and had much greater difficulty in Africa.

A mystery remains: Why has Europe (with its American pro-
longation) been the cradle of this economic revolution while

China had advanced it by several centuries in technical invention (including the invention of printing, achieved five centuries before it appeared in Europe) and while Islam had taught Europe its science around the year 1,000? The answer to such a question is always incomplete and questionable. David S. Landes takes the risk of proposing an answer in his landmark book, *Richesse et pauvreté des nations*.[4] Radically simplifying his thesis, the answer is the following: China had too much state; Islam had too much religion. In both cases individual initiatives were opposed or suffocated.

In Europe Christianity did not have the same effect for three apparent reasons: First, it was inscribed in the Jewish tradition where God entrusted humanity with the management of creation; second, it distinguished religious from political power, creating a new space in which the individual could experiment; third, it distinguished the spirit from the letter, which created a second space for experimentation and innovation. Nothing is changed by the fact that the Catholic Church had Giordano Bruno executed, that it condemned Galileo, or that it had opposed the process of democratization. It carried a message—which it had the merit to never so disfigure that it lost all of its revolutionary power—that it placed every human being in the position to innovate. John Paul II has transcribed this message into numerous texts. In *Laborem Exercens* (1981) he wrote: "In the words of divine revelation, we find deeply inscribed the fundamental truth that humanity, created in God's image, participates by his work in the work of the Creator."[5] In *Centesimus Annus* (1991) he says: "Not being an ideology, the Christian faith in no way seeks to enclose the changing social and political reality in the framework of a rigid morality. It admits that the life of humanity is manifest in history in many diverse and imperfect ways."[6] How can we not see in such positions a reflection of the intuitions of Pierre Teilhard de Chardin?

After the great discoveries, the second phase of the acceleration of globalization occurred in the second part of the nineteenth

century, with the liberalization of commercial trade, the construction of colonial empires, and the girdling of the planet by a network of railroads and canals. From 1820 to 1913, per capita
revenue grew three times more quickly than during the period
1700–1820. This occurred primarily in Great Britain and conti-
nental Europe. English exports, for example, increased by 3.9%
per annum, twice as fast as the growth of production. The British
Empire contained 52 million members in Africa, 330 million in
Asia (primarily in India), and 18 million in America and Oceania.
In sum, the British Empire concerned approximately 400 million
human beings, nearly one person out of three. The Cobden-Che-
valier Treaty of 1860 illustrates the process of liberation of trade.
The first steamboat dates from 1812. In 1880, one can go from
Europe to New York in ten days. The railroad appears in Great
Britain in 1826. In 1913 one million kilometers of railroad encir-
cle the world. The installation of telegraph wires begins in 1850;
that is completed as the first telephone wires are installed in 1913.
Keynes describes the situation of an Englishman (obviously affluent!) on the eve of the First World War: "A Londoner, sweet-
ening his tea as he lay abed, could order different products of the
world by telephone. At the same time and by the same means
he could gamble his wealth in commodities or in a new business
anywhere in the world. He could instantly find a comfortable and
inexpensive means of transportation to go to any country, without
having to show a passport or submit to any formalities."[7]

If we compare the volume of commercial trade (importations
and exportations as a percentage of production) of several great
nations in 1913 and in 1995, we notice that it was scarcely lower
at the beginning of the twentieth century than it is today (approximately 40%), except for the United States, where it has doubled,
moving from 10% to 20%. But in the interval this percentage
collapsed, sometimes by half, due to wars and other crises. Globalization is not linear. It can suddenly regress without these mo-
mentary regressions destroying this evolution through the

centuries. What is the nature of the phase of acceleration we witness today?

Three related phenomena determine the outline of this new step of globalization. First of all, there is the long period of trade liberalization inaugurated after the Second World War by the creation of international institutions that gave themselves the objective of promoting this liberation: the International Monetary Fund, GATT (later the World Trade Organization), OCDE, the Common Market, etc. Moreover, the fall of communism in Europe in the last decade of the century opened new territories to the liberalization of trade, turning the market economy into a universal norm. Finally, the new industrial revolution (based on computers and telecommunications), which at its start was called "a solution that hasn't found its problem," has developed new tools for this extension of markets.

Several figures measure the depth of this change. Between 1920 and 1990, the cost of maritime transportation has been reduced by 70%. Between 1930 and 1990, that of air transportation fell by 84%. The cost of a three-minute telephone call from New York to London was 150% less expensive in 2000 than in 1960. The price of computers (of comparable performance) has been reduced by nearly 2000% during the past forty years. Daily financial transactions in the world are 50 times more important than commercial transactions. Direct investments abroad (excluding portfolio investments) are growing twice as fast as commercial exchanges, which are themselves growing twice as fast as the rate of productivity.

Differing from what we observed in previous stages of globalization, the current stage concerns all nations. The most striking case is that of China, which held itself apart from the great discoveries of the sixteenth century as it did from the liberalization of the nineteenth. Until 1978 the external commerce of China was negligible. It went from 8.5% in 1978 to 36.5% in 1999 (this figure still refers to the sum of exportations and importations related to national production). Long closed to foreign capital,

China is from now on the leading destination of this capital outside the rich nations.

International firms multiply. All the great industries sell their products to and draw their provisions from the entire world. Small firms create obstacles for them. Toyota opens a plant in Valenciennes. Renault purchases Nissan. Daimler takes over Chrysler. Moulinex closes its factories in Normandy because its microwave ovens made in Shanghai are much less expensive. Thirty billion electronic messages are sent each day in the world; none were sent twenty years ago; 60 billion will be sent in five years.

What distinguishes this globalization in the twenty-first century from the globalization in the sixteenth and nineteenth centuries? First, it directly affects everyone. The manual worker of the Renaissance who saw nothing beyond an area of five kilometers has surrendered his place to the most isolated inhabitants of our planet, who receive news of the entire world by turning on the radio or television. At the very moment at which the event occurs, they know that an airplane has crashed into the towers of Manhattan. Never before in the history of humanity has every human being, regardless of location or identity, been the spectator of the collective adventure of the human species at the very moment at which it is occurring. Every human being now knows that he or she belongs to this collectivity, even if he or she feels powerless to change it.

The second difference is that this globalization forces those responsible for this collective life to reflect on its durability. Everyone expects to be able to profit—or at least that his immediate descendants will profit—from the fruits of the economy, such as they appear in the most advanced countries. Take the case of the automobile, which every human being dreams of possessing one day. Today approximately 800 million private cars are in circulation. If all of humanity were equipped as the French are (30 million cars in circulation, because a third of us have more than one car), there would have to be 3 billion cars in the world. In the opinion of experts, this is impossible because of the facts of pollution. Such a situation would lead to the asphyxiation of humanity. For the first time we are forced to face the problem of "sustainable development" and thus to face the issue of the management of our natural environment. Ecology is not one political option among others. It is an inevitable part of all politics. The problem is that it is often unmanageable at the level where political authority is organized, that is, at the level of the national state.

Here appears the major problem at the beginning of this century: the contradiction between the globalization of the economy and the fragmentation of the political. In face of the globalization that underscores our powerlessness, we resist by affirming our social identities in religious, ethnic, cultural, and political terms. After the First World War, the League of Nations counted thirty members; after the Second World War, the United Nations counted fifty; today it counts nearly 200 (the 190th member who just joined is none other than Switzerland, a symbolic act in itself). Each of these national states believes itself to be sovereign while it is only an atom in an ensemble that supports it.

Resistance to globalization rises in the same way. It forces humanity to organize itself outside the limits of the national state, which constitutes the natural framework for collective life—only since a few centuries, one or two in most cases. Now we must reinvent a civic unit for the management of local life and an empire for the harmony of the whole. This is what today we call regionalization and federalism. The European experiment for the past half-century is the most realized of these efforts. Moreover, globalization creates new inequalities both between the North and the South and in the interior of both ensembles. It's the mechanical effect of all acceleration; it aggravates the distances among the groups that undergo it. According to a recent Report on Development in the World by the United Nations (2001 edition), the scale of revenues in the world between the richest 10% and the poorest 10% is from 1 to 60 (1 to 3 in Europe, 1 to 6 in the United States). In the last twenty-five years, per capita income has risen by 5% per annum in China, 3.2% in India, and 2% in the OCDE nations. Thus the distances are being reduced between great human masses. But the distances are growing with sub-Saharan Africa, where per capita income has declined, as it has in central and Eastern Europe. Although in the space of thirty years life expectancy has been prolonged by eight years in the developing countries, it has been shortened in twenty African nations particularly devastated by AIDS; in six of them it has even declined by seven years. Access to potable water has multiplied five-fold in thirty years in the developing countries, but this has not changed the fact that a billion human beings still do not have access to a safe source of water. The fact that the average income in the developing nations has in fact doubled in the last quarter of the twentieth century does not change the fact that 1.2 billion human beings must survive with less than a euro each day and that 2.8 must survive with less than two euros each day. Similarly we still count approximately 325 million children without schooling and 250 million children employed in production.

The new reality is that these inequalities are known, measured, and discussed. Despite all the insufficiencies of the efforts of redistribution of wealth at the world level, this question is officially raised and debated, which was not the case previously. The commitments made are rarely maintained. In the 1970s the rich nations had promised to consecrate 0.7% of their revenues to public assistance to poor nations before the end of the century; we are only at 0.23%. Bitten by remorse, the rich nations decided to fill a part of the delay by reaching 0.5% by the end of the decade. Solidarity does not advance very quickly but it is publicly debated not only as a duty but also as a benefit for everyone. This is the "win-win" mentality which we derive from the primacy of the economic in our collective life. In the nineteenth century it was still completely natural for the strong to live off the pillage of the weak and for the victors to enrich themselves by ruining the vanquished. We clearly see that it is those nations that open themselves the most to trade who make the quickest progress. During the last quarter of a century a hundred nations have made clear progress on the path of democratization. Truly free trade is never without consequences for public liberties. Montesquieu had already written of "sweet trade."

As long as the world has such gaps in development, these gaps will provoke new movements of migration. One of the characteristics of the current phase of globalization is the fact that until now it has not been accompanied by large demographic displacements, which is contrary to what occurred in the earlier phases. The number of migrants at the beginning of the twenty-first century is estimated at approximately 150 million.[8] Net migration (entries minus departures) to the developed countries has been 2.4 million persons per annum during the period 1990–2000. At the head of the countries of immigration is the United States (1.1 million per annum during the last decade of the century), followed by Germany (359,000 per annum), Russia (320,000), Canada (141,400), Italy (116,100), and Singapore (61,800). France has a rate of immigration among Europe's weakest (55,000 per annum). The percentage of foreigners in the population varies between 2 and 10% in the industrialized nations: 10% in the United States, 8.9% in Germany, 5.6% in France (7.3% if one counts all of the residents born abroad). In sum the current migrations are minimal in comparison with the migrations in the past: 20 million Africans displaced toward the Americas and into the Arab world; 51 million Europeans emigrating during the nineteenth and early twentieth centuries toward America, Oceania, and the old colonies; the forced exodus caused by the two world wars.

In the current phase of globalization, the movement of persons has not witnessed the acceleration that has marked the movement of goods, technology, capital, and business. This will not last because we are going to witness a major phenomenon that is going to dominate the twenty-first century: the conjunction of a demographic implosion in the North and a demographic explosion in the South. In Europe the total population may return in fifty years to the level it had fifty years ago; that is to say, it may fall by 200 million inhabitants compared with a current total of 750 million, if fertility does not improve. Even if the percentage of the poor in the world is declining, it remains quite high: 28% of the world population in 1990, 24% in 1999, outside of China; in this last country, the decline has been the strongest: 32% in 1990, 17% in 1999 (these statistics must still undergo further critical analysis, although they have been released by the World Bank). We should remember that the threshold of "monetary poverty" is defined as being half of the average revenue, that is, the revenue that separates a population into two equal parties. The management of the plurality of cultures and religions at the interior of the same nation will be one of the thorniest problems we will face during the new century. This will be so even if the fall of fertility is world-wide and if it appears to be swifter in the poor nations in the twenty-first century than it has been in the rich nations during the nineteenth and twentieth centuries. Thirty years ago, the fertility rate was 5.4 children per woman in the poor countries; today it is 3.1. It is 1.5 in Europe, but to arrive at this figure the Europeans took two hundred years.

3. Christianity's Second Chance

The third phase of acceleration of globalization is one that forces us to imagine multinational institutions (regional and world-wide) capable of mandating rules imposed on all, with sanctions for those who do not respect them. It's the first time that this type of globalization has become visible to everyone, on every continent, and for every condition. It's also the first time that it establishes a direct relation—as the very condition of its survival—between the nature of the physical universe and the culture of living humanity. It is through this more elevated degree of universalization, with its stronger convergence of actions and greater consciousness of our responsibilities, that the current globalization is waiting for us to give it its direction and its meaning.

These conditions might make us wonder if globalization does not constitute a "second chance" for Christianity. As the Roman Empire was once a means of expansion in the first centuries, Christianity can now find in globalization the opportunity to extend and deepen itself. Here is where Teilhard's thought manifests all of its fertility. He knew how to find in modern culture the words and the concepts which permit us to understand this adequation—which we must always renew—between the evangelical message and contemporary realities.

"The Christic," written in March 1955 on the eve of his death, is considered to be Teilhard's spiritual testament. In it, he writes: "Far from losing its primacy in the midst of this vast religious melee, unleashed by the totalization of the modern world, Christianity retakes and consolidates its axial and directive place in the lead of human psychic energies."[9] Teilhard argues that in no other "credo" can one find the following characteristics of the Christian God: historical insertion by Christ into the process of evolution; universal expansion of this "Christic" center by the mediation of the resurrection; the power to integrate into one body the totality of the human race. He writes: "In the end, what makes unconquerable the superiority of Christianity over all other types of faith is its increasingly conscious identification with a 'christogenesis,' that is to say with a perceived rise of a certain universal presence." The Christian sees God as a center that seeks a sphere and he or she sees the world as the sphere that seeks a center. Christ emerges when the universe converges. "A religion of evolution is what in the end humanity more and more explicitly needs for the sake of survival and an abundant life."

Naturally we see in these considerations a reflection of the historical debates during Teilhard's youth over the relationship between the evolution of species and the teaching of the Church. But the elaboration of Teilhard's thought permits us today to offer a better translation of the deep core of the Christian message into the language of our time, without ceding to the temptation of turning *The Human Phenomenon* (the most accomplished work of the author) into some kind of "fifth gospel." Such idolatry would make no sense to Teilhard himself, who wrote: "Of course (I know it only too well), despite the ambitious splendor of my ideas, I remain in fact marked by a disturbing imperfection. In spite of the pretensions of its formulation, my faith does not produce in me enough real charity or the calm confidence that the children's catechism produces in the person kneeling next to me." This admission in no way alters his conviction expressed in the last lines of this astonishing text: "In this moment everywhere on the earth, at the center of the new spiritual atmosphere created by the apparition of the idea of evolution, floats in a state of extreme mutual intensity both the love of God and faith in the world." Others might say the love of the world and faith in God.

Another dimension of this double extension of Christianity in time and space is the ecumenical dimension. I borrow from Pastor Konrad Raiser, general secretary of the Ecumenical Council of Churches, some reflections on the future of Christianity in globalization.[10] He says: "There exists a profound relationship between globalization and the universal vision of Christianity. . . . The ecumenical movement, with its commitment not only to the unity of Christians but just as strongly to the unity of humanity, can even be considered as one of the factors that have brought about this new global consciousness. In the face of globalization, Christianity should be both encouraging and vigilant. It cannot be satisfied with a human community founded on domination, accumulation, and competition; its role is to recall the demands of mutuality, of sufficiency (in the sense of moderation), and of cooperation." The Church must make a critical analysis of the forms of globalization, while being vigilant not to simply dismiss this process because of its flaws. Pastor Raiser adds: "At the base of its tradition of catholicity and of conciliarity [this is a Protestant speaking], Christianity can make an important contribution to the intercultural dialogue at the interior of the Christian community as well as between Christians and their neighbors of other religions."

Globalization is thus a "second chance" for Christianity because it offers the methods of supplementary diffusion (thanks to computers and telecommunications), and because it opens for it new territories, especially in Asia, where most of the great human masses who do not know the gospel live. More importantly, Christians should be able to critique and find a message in globalization. The Christian religion is the most extended in the world if one counts the billion Catholics with the billion Christians of other churches. This is one of three persons in the world. It is true that Islam is progressing more rapidly: 12% of the population at the beginning of the twentieth century, 19% today (approximately 1.2 billion people). But it is increasing primarily in nations that believe themselves the victims of globalization, in which they see a modern form of cultural and economic colonialism. This will be less and less true with the accession of new countries to the rank of developed economies, such as India, China, and Turkey. Islam's extension will suffer because of the status it gives to women and its confusion of the political with the religious. Traditional Asian beliefs (Hinduism, Buddhism) are more of a type of wisdom than of a religion, which would seem to make them consonant enough with modern mentalities. But they are so tied to specific Asian cultures that they are difficult to export.

The "desacralization" of the world is perhaps not as obvious as we claim in France. It is true that the churches have emptied out, baptisms have declined by half since the war, and new priests are ten times less numerous. But don't we have the nostalgic tendency to gild the Christianity of traditional societies where the institutional framework took the place of Christian witness? We refer to Louis XIV as "most Christian," but he was allied with the Great Turk and massacred women and children in the Palatinate in the seventeenth century. Christianity is no longer the framework of our nations, it is a source. Perhaps it is less visible but it is not necessarily less effective in incarnating its message. We still have the duty to keep clear the path of the source when it is invaded by noxious weeds. If the source is lost, the river will become polluted. The risk of a soft ideology, vaguely inspired by Christian values, is a lost identity. In this situation people speak about nonviolence, equal rights, solidarity, and tolerance, but without connecting these good intentions to the principles that gave rise to them. We risk seeing them disappear in the first tempest.

Christianity can provide us with a better comprehension of globalization. More than a new mode of trade, it is a step in the realization of God's plan for the world. God has had the folly to confide a part of this realization of the plan to a free, thus fallible, creature: humanity. The space in which we live and work will have its "natural" end: roasted by the sun in 5 billion years, emptied of the human species in four hundred years if fertility does not increase, or destroyed by the explosion of a meteor at some undetermined moment. We know nothing of this but we do know that God has asked us to begin the construction of the Kingdom starting now in the knowledge that we will not be the ones to finish it. This is built on the truth that a Christian is not only a human being who believes in God, but a human being who knows that God believes in humanity.

Translated by John J. Conley, S.J.

Teilhard and Science

CHAPTER 8

The Emergence of Consciousness in Biological Evolution and Quantum Reality

Lothar Schäfer

Twentieth-century physics has shown that reality is different from what we had thought. At the foundation of ordinary things, elementary particles are not as real as the things that they form, but they are different in essence. Physical reality is not what it looks like, and it is possible to propose that:

1. The basis of the material world is nonmaterial.

2. Reality has the nature of an indivisible, non-separable wholeness.

3. Quantum entities possess properties of consciousness in a rudimentary way.

These aspects of physical reality provide an important framework for the vision of Teilhard de Chardin, which had no basis in the outgoing mechanistic-materialistic worldview of the science of his time. At the same time, quantum reality is the basis for a new view of biological evolution.

1. Some Characteristic Aspects of Quantum Reality

1. The Basis of the Material World Is Nonmaterial

Schrödinger's Quantum Mechanics is currently the only effective theory which serves as a basis of calculating the properties of molecules from first principles. In this theory, the electrons in atoms are not tiny particles, little balls of matter, but they are standing waves, wave patterns, or mathematical forms. We owe to Max Born the discovery that the nature of these waves is that of probability waves.

Probabilities are dimensionless numbers. Probability waves are empty; they carry no mass or energy, just information on numerical relations. Nevertheless, all visible order in the universe is determined by the interference of such waves. For example, the wave functions of atoms determine what kind of molecules can be formed and what kind of chemistry they afford; the wave functions of molecules, in turn, determine the intermolecular interactions which are the basis of the general properties of materials and, in particular, of the chemistry of living cells. In this way we find that the order of the world is based on nonmaterial principles. The basis of the order of the material world is nonmaterial.

In contemporary physics such conclusions were unexpected, but now they are not. Pythagoras had already thought that "all things are numbers" and he claimed that "the harmony of the cosmos is based on the ratios of numbers." But what are probabilities? Ratios of numbers! Similarly, in his *Timaeus*, Plato proposed that atoms are mathematical forms, and St. Augustine wrote: "The older I got, the more despicable became the emptiness of my thought, because I could think of no entity in any other way than as bodily visible."[1]

2. The Nonlocality or Non-separability of Reality

The non-separability of reality has been revealed by experiments in which elementary particles act on each other without delay over long distances. Experiments testing Bell's Theorem and their interpretations (Bell, 1965, 1988; Aspect et al. 1981, 1982; d'Espagnat, 1981; Shimony, 1991) have shown that, under certain conditions, decisions made by an observer in one laboratory may have an instantaneous effect on the outcome of experiments performed in another laboratory, an arbitrarily long distance away.[2] Two particles, which at one time interact and then move away from each other, can stay connected and act as though they were one thing, no matter how far apart they are. This phenomenon defines the nonlocality of the quantum world.

If the nature of reality is nonlocal, it is an indivisible wholeness. In that case, Kafatos and Nadeau (1990) proposed, a remarkable conclusion can be drawn: Since our consciousness has emerged out of this wholeness and is part of it, it is possible to infer that an element of consciousness is active in the universe: *cosmic consciousness.*

3. Aspects of Mind

To physically affect a thing, we must spend some energy. For example, to move an object from one place to another we have to push it; that is, impart some energy to it. Just thinking about such an action will not get it done.

Elementary particles, again, are different. Under certain conditions they change their behavior when what we know about them changes. They react to gradients of information, as though what we may think about them can affect them. In single-particle interference experiments, for example, *which-way information* destroys coherence.

In the ordinary world of our sense experience, the only known entity which can react to the flow of information is a conscious mind. In this sense we can say that, at the foundation of reality, *entities with mind-like properties are found.* Polkinghorne called this "causality through active information."[3]

"It is not unreasonable to imagine," Wheeler wrote, "that information sits at the core of physics, just as it sits at the core of a computer."[4] In passing a system of slits, electrons seem to *know* how many of them are open and how many closed, and they adjust their behavior accordingly. In a vacuum, pairs of particles can appear out of nothing, provided they exist for such a short time that we cannot *know* for sure that they existed. A particle that forms a singlet state with another particle seems to *know* whether or not a measurement was made on its twin, a long distance away. For Stapp, "the central mystery of quantum theory is 'how does information get around so quick? How does the particle know that there are two slits? How does the information about what is happening everywhere else get collected to determine what is likely to happen here? How does the particle know that it was looked for in some far-away place and not found?'"[5] And Wiener emphasized: "Information is information, not matter or energy. No materialism which does not admit this can survive at the present day."[6]

From the mind-like aspects of elementary particles Eddington generalized: "The universe is of the nature of a thought or sensation in a universal Mind . . . the stuff of the world is mind-stuff."[7] And for Jeans: "Mind no longer appears as an accidental intruder into the realm of matter; we are beginning to suspect that we ought rather to hail it as the creator and governor of the realm of matter."[8]

It is in many phenomena that aspects of consciousness come to the fore: nonmaterial probability waves are closer to the nature of a thought than that of a thing. The limited capacity of electronic states to store electrons is the basis of all of chemistry and of the visible order of the universe. It is the result, not of any mechanical force that we know, but of a mental principle; namely, the symmetry of the wave functions of elementary particles—i.e., the symmetry of numbers. "There is indeed something quasi-mental, nonphysical about it," Margenau wrote.[9]

In quantum jumps, quantum systems act spontaneously. A conscious mind is the only entity that we know that can act in this way. Spontaneity in physics is absence of causality. This "leaves us," Eddington wrote: "with no clear distinction between the Natural and the Supernatural."[10]

Thus, at the quantum level of reality, the line of demarcation is blurred between the Natural and the Supernatural; between the physical and the metaphysical; and between the mental and the material. The impression is unavoidable that quantum reality is a transcendent reality, as different from ordinary reality as it is beyond direct observation. At the level of elementary particles, idea-like states become matter-like. The Word is becoming flesh. As whatever King Midas touched turned into gold, whatever we observe turns into matter. At its frontiers, observable reality does not fade into nothing but into something invisible. Physical reality borders on the metaphysical. In the same way in which dead atoms form living organisms and stupid molecules form intelligent brains, metaphysical entities form physical reality.

2. *The Importance of Virtual States for the Emergence of Complex Order in the Universe*

In his book, *Finding Darwin's God*, Miller writes: "In a scientific sense, it is certainly true that the world runs according to material rules, that we are material beings, and that our biology works by means of the laws of physics and chemistry. To all of this, evolution added one important fact—namely that our biological *origins* are material as well."[11] Similarly, referring to a quotation by the evolutionary biologist Douglas Futumya, Miller writes: "Science, by this analysis, is mechanism and materialism. And all that Darwin did was to show that mechanism and materialism applied to biology, too."[12]

In contrast to the current views of mainstream biology my thesis here is that science is *not* materialism and it is *not* the kind of mechanism which was accessible to Darwin. It is true that biology is ruled by the laws of physics and chemistry, but these laws can no longer be understood within the framework of traditional materialism and mechanism. Rather, since molecules are the basis of life and are quantum systems, no comprehensive view of the emergence of complex order in the biosphere is possible without taking the quantum properties of molecules into account. Quantum reality is the basis of all visible phenomena.

1. First Evolutionary Relevant Aspect of the Quantum World: The No-Copy, No-Error, Just Quantum Jumping Account of Biological Evolution

All molecules exist in quantum states. All that a molecule can do is to jump from one state to the next. Quantum jumps are spontaneous, have no known cause, and are ruled by transition probabilities, which depend on the wave functions of the states involved. When processes are ruled by probabilities, one can never be sure of the outcome of a specific event.

In living cells, the synthesis of genes—DNA molecules—is a quantum process. That is, one can never be sure of the outcome of a specific case. When a particular stretch of DNA is synthesized, the probability is overwhelming that the product sequence of nucleotides is the same as that of an attending DNA catalyst, but that *need* not be so. When the product is not the same as the attending DNA, we say an *error* was made in *copying* a gene, and a *mutation* occurred.

In contrast, quantum entities make no copies and they make no errors, they just populate quantum states. In the synthesis of DNA a group of nucleotides simply populates a common quantum state. In a mutation a group of nucleotides populates a vacant state which was not occupied before. If the new state causes variations in phenotype, then natural selection will take control.

In this way one is led away from mainstream biology and to the view that the units of natural selection are not stretches of chromosomes but the quantum states which actualize in chromosomes. If identical DNA molecules are not copies of one another, but just repeated actualizations of the same quantum state, the concept of descent changes its meaning. In a way, species do not change, but genes change quantum states. Since the quantum states that give rise to living organisms have not descended from one another, their phenotypic effects have not descended either, one from the other.

2. Second Evolutionary Relevant Aspect of the Quantum World: The Importance of Virtual States

In the center of all processes of emergence in the universe we find *virtual states*. Every quantum system consists not only of the state in which it is observed, but also of countless other, invisible states that are vacant. When a particular molecule is observed in the state that it occupies, other states also exist, but they are not real in a material sense, because they are empty. In general, all things contain countless empty states.

Quantum chemists call empty states *virtual states*. They virtually exist, but not really, like ordinary (actual) things. Virtual states are mathematical forms, bits of information, but they are more than the mere idea of a mathematical form, *because they can become real, when a system jumps into them.* They can be termed *Heisenberg objects*; i.e., entities which exist "between the idea of a thing and a real thing."[13]

The hydrogen molecule can serve as a simple example (fig. 1). When the wave functions of the most stable states of two hydrogen atoms (the $H1s$ states) interfere with each other, two molecular states are formed, one of which ($1s$) has an energy below, the other one ($1s^*$) above the $H1s$-energy of the isolated atoms. In the ground state of H_2, the two electrons of the molecule occupy the lower state, leaving the upper one *empty* or *virtual*.

In addition to the virtual state created by the interference of $H1s$ states, the quantum structure of H_2 contains many more empty states (not shown in figure 1) because the H-atoms contain themselves virtual states, which can be thought to interfere and create additional molecular states. This is a peculiar situation: The interference of virtual atomic states, entities not real in a

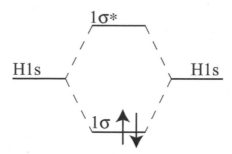

Figure 1. **Energy diagram for molecular states formed in the hydrogen molecule, H_2, from atomic $H1s$ states.** If the wave functions of the 1s-states of two hydrogen atoms ($H1s$) interfere with each other, two molecular states or molecular orbitals are formed, whose energies are *below* (1σ) or *above* ($1\sigma^*$) the $H1s$-energy of the isolated atoms. If the two electrons occupy the lower 1σ-state with antiparallel spin orientations (symbolized by the arrows), a system results that is more stable than two non-bonded atoms.

material sense, creates molecular virtual states, again not quite real, but nevertheless with a predictable mathematical order which is predetermined by the conditions of the system and has the potential to actualize.

When a molecule occupies a virtual state, that state is actualized. At that point virtual order becomes actual order. In this way the actualization of virtual order in quantum jumps appears as a simple mechanism by which a transcendent order in the universe can express itself in the material world. All molecules, indeed all systems, the universe included, are centers of potentiality, of virtual states which form a realm of potentia in physical reality, from which something new is constantly emerging.

3. Virtual States as Parmenidian Entities

Virtual states can be considered as Parmenidian entities. Parmenides believed that motion is possible only, if empty space exists, into which an object can move. Since he also believed that there is no empty space, he claimed that there can be no motion. Quantum systems confirm and refine the Parmenidian principle: A system needs empty (virtual) states in order to be able to change.

Quantum virtual states exist in the state space of a system. Their order does not reside in observable forms, but in virtual functions. The virtual wave functions are pieces of a transcendent order.

The description above focused on the formation of molecular electronic states as a simple example. In addition, many other types of states exist which make up the total state of a system; they control the conditions of translational, vibrational, and rotational motion in space, and of the motion of chemical species across surfaces of potential energy, which leads them from one synthetic ensemble to another. In each case a given system is observed in just one actual total state of its state space, while many others exist which are empty. Every empty state carries with it a well-defined wave form, a pattern of order and information, but a virtual pattern, a piece of transcendence—not quite a part of the material world, but always ready to enter it. The universe bristles with empty states that have not yet provoked an actual event and, transcribing a statement by Wheeler, it seems safe to say that it is filled with more virtuality than actuality. In an incessant, restless dance, occupied states are constantly abandoned and become virtual, while empty states become occupied and real. At the foundation of things transcendent order and real order are interlocked in an uninterrupted frantic embrace. From the transcendent to the real, from the real to the transcendent—that is how easy that is.

Genes, i.e., DNA molecules, are not exempt from this general state of matter. For each chain of nucleotides, there is a high density of empty states, and finite probabilities for transitions into each of them. A mutation is the actualization of a virtual state of a gene.

4. Virtual Cosmic States as Platonic Ideas

Virtual states can also be viewed as Platonic ideas. The entire universe is a quantum system. Its occupied states form the visible part of reality. In addition, there are infinitely many cosmic virtual states. Since they are not real in the material sense, the order that they define is a transcendent cosmic order, and *virtual-state actualization* (VSA) is the mechanism by which the material world is secreted and separated from the wholeness of the transcendent order of the universe.

If the nature of the universe is that of a wholeness, all states are cosmic states, and even the quantum states of single molecules are a part of the one whole cosmic quantum structure. Thus, molecular states can be thought to exist in the virtual-cosmic-state space before the corresponding molecules exist as actual lumps of matter. Chances are that the quantum states which actualize in DNA already existed at a time when the real DNA molecules did not yet exist as material lumps on this planet. Since, in the quantum reality, everything that can happen at some time must happen, given a sufficient length of time, the actualization of states which express themselves in life forms was inevitable. Since we have to assume that the virtual-state space extends through cosmic wholeness, as though it existed beyond space-time, there is no reason to believe that the emergence of life was restricted to a single point in time, or to a single locality, like our planet.

One is thus led in a natural way to Teilhard's view of life as a phenomenon that "cannot be considered in the Universe any longer as a superficial accident but, rather, must be considered to be under strong pressure everywhere—ready to burst from the smallest crack no matter where in the universe—and, once actualized, it is incapable of not using every opportunity and means to arrive at the extreme of its potentiality, externally of Complexity, and internally of Consciousness."[14]

In the virtual-state space of the universe, it is sufficient that each quantum state exists only once, like in a central library or in the world of Plato's ideas. Out of the single system of quantum states representing a hydrogen atom in the cosmic library, the countless H-atoms which exist as material particles are repeated actualizations: a single state (or coherent group of states) in the virtual library; multiplicity in the visible order of the material world. In the virtual order, Ockham's razor ranks supreme and Cartesian clarity is the ultimate principle. In this model of the universal order, it is considered that there is a nucleus of cosmic virtual states, like a central archive or processing unit, from which the material world emerges by VSA. There is wholeness in the virtual order, separateness in the actualized objects. Our world has lost the sense of wholeness, because it is filled with repeated actualizations of the same virtual quantum states.

The notion that identical material structures are repeated actualizations of the same virtual quantum state conveys a different view of things than the contention that they are copies of one another. The notion of copies and errors of mainstream biology represents the naïve view of genetic processes. Like other anthropocentric views, it will eventually have to be abandoned. The reference point of a gene is not another gene, but a virtual quantum state. In a pool of identical genes, we consider none as the copy of another, but all as the actualizations of the same cosmic quantum state. Arbitrary numbers of identical DNA molecules are produced from a single quantum state of the cosmic library, a single bit of the virtual universal order.

5. *The Emergence of Biological Complexity through Virtual-State Actualization*

By the concept of emergence we mean the becoming, or coming into being, of systems for which there are no antecedents. Emergence refers to the appearance of something new. Something appears in the material world that did not exist before, like new life forms in biology.

The process of becoming has often been considered as enigmatic. How is it possible that never-before-existing complex systems spontaneously emerge from simpler ones? Since the root of such processes is not found in visible forms, Darwinians have often claimed that complex biological systems are the result of nothing but chance and appear out of nothing. Since miraculous

appearances out of nothing and order from chaos do not correspond to our normal experience of the nature of things, it is suggested that the creation of complex structures by VSA is
immensely more satisfactory because it has a well-established empirical precedent: At the molecular level, the emergence of complex order from actualizations of a coherent virtual order is so
commonplace that it is a trivial phenomenon. Molecules do not
create complex order *de nihilo*, but out of their virtual states.

For Teilhard, "the primacy accorded to the psychic and to
thought in the stuff of the universe" was a main theme of his
vision.[15] This view is now finding some foundation in the VSA
hypothesis, in that virtual states are mind-like, not matter-like.
Cosmic virtual states are ultimately expressions of the mind-like
background of the universe which may be the source not only
of the principles needed to construct our bodies, but also of the
universal principles that make up our mind.

This brings out an important difference between Darwinism
and the quantum perspective of biological evolution that is proposed here. In contrast to Darwinism, the VSA hypothesis assumes the existence of an underlying nonmaterial and coherent
order to all of reality, a realm of potentiality which is at the same
time *immanent*, because it is contained in the things, and *transcendent*, because it is not stored in visible forms and part of a virtual
cosmic structure. Chance plays a role in both models. But in Darwinism the evolving order is created by chance, a *"noise"* that natural selection will transform into *"music."*[16] In the emergence by
VSA, the music is part of an ongoing cosmic concert which is
revealed in quantum jumps. Chance lies in the quantum jumping,
whether a jump will occur or not, and where it will lead to. But
the order of the states on which the jumping will land has nothing
to do with chance. Both models agree with the same experimental
evidence, which biologists have accumulated in the course of
time. But only the concept of VSA is in agreement with the general understanding of the quantum nature of molecules and all

material systems. Numerous observations show that the molecules of biology, too, are quantum systems.

6. Evidence for the Need of a Quantum Perspective of Evolution

Against the quantum perspective of evolution[17] it has often been argued that biomolecules are too large to be considered quantum systems and that it is completely sufficient to treat them as dense Newtonian objects. This is the currently accepted view of mainstream biology. In contrast, there is growing evidence that this is not so.

For example, quantum computations of the structures of peptides and proteins[18] have predicted details of protein structures, which were subsequently confirmed by protein crystallography but are absent in computational results obtained by classical modeling procedures. These structural trends represent a clear quantum effect in an important property of proteins.

In quantum calculations of clay minerals,[19] the size of a mineral crystal must be extrapolated to infinity in order to obtain realistic results which are in agreement with experimental data. Such studies show that all systems, regardless of size, can be understood as quantum systems.

Cytochrome oxidase is a giant protein molecule, with a molecular weight of some 400,000 atomic mass units. Its function in electron transfer reactions in living cells has been studied by spectroscopic means.[20] Spectroscopic molecular phenomena always involve the absorption or emission of quanta of light accompanied by transitions of a molecule from one quantum state to another. Such phenomena make it completely impossible to understand cytochrome oxidase as a Newtonian corpuscle.

Apart from such specific experimental observations, one must ask in a general way what the totality or wholeness of the universe might mean for the origin of life. What does the discovery of virtual states in small molecules mean for biological order? What do the mind-like aspects of the background of reality mean for the nature of life that evolves in the biosphere? Such questions are not meaningless because potential answers may not now be amenable to experiment. It seems a greater risk to neglect them than to discuss them.

In statistical analyses, the time available since the birth of this planet has frequently been judged to be not sufficient for a process in which life evolves out of nothing and by random variations.[21] Considerably less time is needed for a process like VSA, in which the complex order already exists in virtual states and is merely *revealed* by chance, compared to a process in which the complex order has to be *created* by chance.

It is one of Darwin's famous postulates that "Nature does not make jumps." In contrast, contemporary physics tells us that nature makes nothing but jumps, namely quantum jumps. As it seems, the overall progression of evolution is not exempted from this law, because the succession of evolutionary levels is frequently not gradual, but "everything seems to have burst into the world ready made."[22]

The theory of *punctuated equilibrium*[23] is an attempt to explain geological observations which show "the geological instantaneous origination and subsequent stability (often for millions of years) of paleontological 'morphospecies.'" Such a process—the rapid and spontaneous change of a system from an enduring equilibrium to a new state—bears all the signatures of a quantum process. Specifically, such a conduct is typically found among systems with crossed quantum states: Sodium iodide, NaI, is a simple example.[24]

When sodium iodide is trapped in one of its molecular states, the temporal sequence of radial probability maxima corresponds to a cyclic movement of the molecule from small distances to large, and back to small.[25] One of the states of NaI, the NaI(o+) state, is crossed by a dissociative state at an Na-I distance of $\sim$720 pm. Every time when the system in its cyclic motion passes the crossing point, there is a spontaneous branching off of a part of the population to a different state and to different chemical species. In modeling calculations of this process[26] the branching is illustrated by a bifurcation of the population.

In this example, populations of molecules display long periods of stasis (residence of a molecular population in the same quantum state) punctuated by short periods of spontaneous transition of a part of the population to a different state and to different chemical species. The analogy to the branching of a vertical lineage in biological evolution by punctuated equilibrium is striking. One begins to suspect that punctuated equilibria in biological change are indicative of the crossing of quantum entities, immensely more complex than the simple model chosen above, from one state to another.

7. *The Importance of Quantum Selection*

The formation of chemical bonds in the course of a mutation is a quantum process. Transitions among quantum states are involved. Because there is a choice between a large number of virtual DNA states, a selection is made in a mutation and differences in transition probabilities will favor the selection of some states over others. This is a form of selection, but it is not natural selection: It can be adequately termed *quantum selection*.

We do not know now the quantum states involved in mutations. Thus, we do not know whether or not quantum selection plays an important role in the process of evolution. This is a most important concept nevertheless, because it shows that natural selection is not acting alone. Natural selection has to drive the progression of evolution in tandem with quantum selection. Even though we do not know the quantum states involved in genetic processes, it is obvious that the evolutionary progression must in some way be affected by their properties.

Quantum selection describes a true quantum effect: Classical randomness and chance can lead to anything. Quantum randomness can lead only from one well-defined state to another well-defined state, and not to an arbitrary point between two states. The hydrogen atom can serve as a simple example (fig. 2).

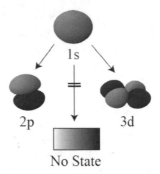

Figure 2. Probability density plots (iso-density surfaces of atomic orbitals) of possible and impossible H-atom electronic states. The probability density of the 1s, 2p, and 3d states are shown. A state with a box-like distribution (center, bottom) does not exist. Graphs of atomic orbitals were generated with the 'Orbital Viewer' Program by David Manthey, http://www.orbitals.com.

A hydrogen atom can make a transition from a state (1s), whose probability density is spherical, to a state (2p) whose probability distribution is approximately bi-spherical, or to a state (3d) with an approximately tetra-spherical distribution (fig. 2). But a hydrogen atom cannot jump into a box (a state whose distribution is that of a box) because such a state does not exist.

Similarly, evolution may have led from fish to amphibians to mammals and human beings. But it has not been able to lead from fish to griffons, to basilisks and humans with wings, because cosmic virtual states do not exist for such mythical beasts.

In summary, when mutations are understood as transitions among quantum states

- the order that evolves in the biosphere is not from nothing but from the actualization of virtual states whose order existed a long time before it was actualized;
- the concept of descent changes its meaning;
- a second selection mechanism, quantum selection, must be considered, which drives evolution in tandem with natural selection;

- The center of evolutionary activity is shifted from the material level to the level of quantum entities, whose mind-like properties may force us to think that quantum reality is not only the source of the physical principles needed to construct our bodies, but also of principles related to our minds;

Reductionism in science is the claim that one principle exists that can provide a basis for explaining all phenomena in the universe. In contemporary biology everything is reduced to the properties of genes. This is halfway reductionism.

Genes, lumps of matter, are not the terminus of reality. They are not the authors of any information, just vehicles (inverting Dawkins' term) by which the messages of a deeper order are revealed. They are agents of an underlying order, the order of quantum reality. Through genes, the (virtual) order of quantum reality can express itself in the material world.

Sociobiologists and ethologists claim that our values, including our moral values, are adaptations constructing our minds. In "The Evolution of Ethics," Ruse and Wilson write: "Morality, or more strictly our belief in morality, is merely an adaptation put in place to further our reproductive ends. Hence the basis of ethics does not lie in God's will—or in the metaphysical roots of evolution or any other part of the framework of the Universe. In an important sense, ethics as we understand it is an illusion fobbed off on us by our genes to get us to cooperate. It is without external grounding. . . . The way our biology enforces its ends is by making us think that there is an objective higher code, to which we are all subject."[27] Similarly, Ruse writes: "Where I start, with great enthusiasm, is with Charles Darwin's theory of evolution through natural selection. This leads me to the conclusion that our morality is put in place, by our biology, to make us good social animals. . . . I do not accept objective moral properties. . . . Morality is a collective illusion of humankind, put in place by our genes in order to make us good cooperators."[28]

In the quantum world, the actions of genes are not driven by any purpose but, following the laws of physics and chemistry, they reveal universal order. Genes are not great deceivers of humanity, not selfish impostors, they are just messengers and relay stations by which information from deep inside reality is transmitted to us.

Evolutionary psychologists claim that all human behaviors are adaptations. If behavior is an adaptation, it means that we were selected for it. If morality is an illusion set up by our genes, we were all selected for a particular type of stupidity—namely the inability to recognize a cheap trick when we see one.

All sensations in material systems are sustained by material processes. The awareness of universal principles in human beings is no exception to that rule. But that does not mean that the principles, such as the moral principles whose awareness in us is possible through material processes, are the *creations* of these processes. Specifically, when the material processes in living cells are thought to have a genetic basis, this does not mean that the principles emerging in our consciousness are *created* by the genes. In the dictionary of Darwinians, "genetic" means "passed on from ancestry." In the quantum perspective of evolution, "genetic" means "expressed from virtual cosmic order."

It seems reasonable to propose that the universal principles which appear in our thinking are reflections of universal order. In that case the adaptation involved in moral behavior is the capacity of the mind to comprehend the significance of universal principles. In the same way in which we evolved the capacity of understanding universal principles in physics, we evolved the capacity for universal principles in ethics.

Like the physics of Newton, the biology of Darwin is not false, but both apply merely to the mechanical surface of things. For a comprehensive interpretation of evolution, Darwin's hypothesis must be supplemented by the quantum properties of matter. Darwinism is steam engine technology applied to the integrated circuits of life.

3. Quantum Reality and the Vision of Teilhard de Chardin

1. Some Characteristic Aspects of Teilhard's Vision of Evolution Amenable to Comparisons with the Quantum Perspective

During the first half of the twentieth century, Teilhard de Chardin developed a theory of evolution whose essential aspects are remarkably consistent with characteristic aspects of quantum reality. One cannot usually find a description of Teilhard's views in textbooks of biology, because they are not testable science. They are fascinating nevertheless, and to many they have become a source of hope. Detailed descriptions can be found in King and Trennert-Hellwig.[29]

In Teilhard's vision as in quantum reality

- an element of consciousness is active at all levels of reality;

- the mental enters the material world in a natural way;

- the visible order of the universe is based on the principles of a transcendent reality.

In Teilhard's view, life is not "a fortuitous accident of terrestrial matter" but "a specific effect of matter turned complex; a property that is present in the entire cosmic stuff. . . ."[30] Therefore, fluid-like, life can be thought to be under pressure to express itself in the material world. If there is such a pressure, it can be thought to be the pressure on virtual states to actualize in material structures.

It is part of Teilhard's view that matter and consciousness are not "two substances" or "two different modes of existence," "but two aspects of the same cosmic stuff."[31] Thus, matter is never really "dead," but should be called "pre-vital."[32] "Everything in nature is basically living, or at least pre-living."[33] This statement is not in contrast to the fact that it was possible to develop a successful mechanistic science of matter because the mental in elementary particles is so attenuated that it does not interfere with

the mechanical.[34] But, in Teilhard's views, that does not mean that
it is absent.

> There is no doubt: the so-called brute matter is certainly ani-
> mated in its own way. . . . Atoms, electrons, molecules, whatever
> they may be if they be anything at all outside of us, must have a
> rudiment of immanence; i.e., a spark of consciousness. Before on
> this planet the physico-chemical conditions allowed the birth of
> organic life, the universe was either not yet anything in itself, or it
> had already formed a nebula of consciousness.[35]

In this way, Teilhard established the "primacy of the psychic and
of thought" in the processes of the universe,[36] in total contrast to
the mechanistic sciences of the classical era. Throughout his writing, "life" is synonymous with "consciousness," the process of
biological evolution is essentially the evolution of a spiritual
sphere, the noosphere, and it is implied that consciousness is the
primary base of all reality. "Life is the rise of consciousness."
Even in the vegetable kingdom, some sort of diffuse psychism
exists, "growing in its own manner."[37]

In human beings, evolution became conscious of itself and the
power of mind became an important driving force. When evolution entered the realm of thinking, when thought and reflection
were born, a totally new development began: "Another world is
born. Abstraction, logic, reasoned choice and inventions, mathematics, art, calculation of space and time, anxieties and dreams of
love—all these activities of *inner life* are nothing else than the
effervescence of the newly formed center as it explodes onto itself."[38]

In the human realm, due to the force of the psychic, "an increasingly dense and energized atmosphere is forming on this
planet of creative and inventive endeavors and efforts; at first just
like a light and thin fog, blown hither and thither by every whim
and imagination; but then like a dense skin, which becomes for-
midably irresistible from that moment on, when a powerful vortex
grips it and forces it to focus . . . in order to thrust forward, like

an arrow, in a commonly fixed direction, to the world of the real, with the purpose, not only to gain a higher level of pleasure or knowledge, but a higher level of being."[39]

When the process of evolution is transferred into the hands of self-conscious beings, it needs a direction and a goal in order to maintain its momentum. "Evolution, by becoming conscious of itself in the depths of ourselves, only needs to look at itself in the mirror to perceive itself in all its depths and to decipher itself. In addition it becomes free to dispose of itself—it can give itself or refuse itself. Not only do we read in our slightest acts the secrets of its proceedings; but for an elementary part *we hold it in our hands*, responsible for its past to its future."[40]

In an evolution that is conscious of itself, there is the danger of the "malady of space-time," the "sickness of the dead end"; and "requirements of the future" are needed to guarantee "a suitable outcome."

> There is a danger that the elements of the world should refuse to serve the world—because they think; or more precisely that the world should refuse itself when perceiving itself through reflection. Under our modern disquiet, what is forming and growing is nothing less than an organic crisis in evolution. . . . Man will never take a step in a direction he knows to be blocked. There lies precisely the ill that causes our disquiet.
>
> Having got so far, what are the minimum requirements to be fulfilled before we can say that the road ahead of us is *open*? There is one, but it is everything. It is that we should be assured the space and the chances to fulfill ourselves, that is to say, to progress (directly or indirectly, individually or collectively) till we arrive at the utmost limits of ourselves.[41]

Teilhard called the goal of evolution the omega point, whose function he thus defined. Guided by consciousness, the goal of humanity is to reach this point, where the Consciousness of humanity will be united with the Consciousness that is active in the universe, marking the end and completion of the empirical process outside of space-time.[42]

If the singular point of convergence of matter, if the omega point is really the keystone in the vault of the noosphere, "then it can be understood only as that point, in which the universe, having reached the limits of its centralization, meets another, even more unfathomable center—a Center that exists out of itself, an absolutely final Principle of irreversibility and personalization: the only true omega. . . . And it is in this point, if I am not totally misled, that the question of God emerges for the science of evolution . . . God as driving force, collection point and guarantor."[43]

2. Transcendent Reality

From the quotation above it appears that Teilhard considered the omega point as the gateway to a transcendent reality outside of space-time. As shown in Part 1, the assumption of such a reality is no longer in conflict with contemporary physics and may even be suggested by it.

We can only speculate and guess what the nature of the transcendent part of reality might be. The signs are that it is mind-like rather than matter-like (Goswami et al., 1993; Kafatos and Nadeau, 1990; Srivastava, 2001, 2002) and that *consciousness, not matter, is the primary reality*. Thus, it is perfectly plausible to think that the completion of the processes of the universe will be the merger of two different streams of consciousness, human and divine.

It is possible to assume that, as envisioned by Teilhard for the omega point, transcendent consciousness resides outside of space-time. In fact, a growing number of physicists are willing to consider phenomena which reside outside of space-time but affect space-time processes. Already in the thirties of the last century, Jeans was inspired by the physics of his time to suggest that "the minutest phenomena of nature do not admit of representation in the space-time framework at all . . . other phenomena can only be represented by going outside the (space-time) continuum. We have, for instance, already tentatively pictured consciousness as something outside the continuum. . . . It is conceivable that happenings entirely outside the continuum determine what we describe as the 'course of events' inside the continuum, and that the apparent indeterminacy of nature may arise merely from our trying to force happenings which occur in many dimensions into a smaller number of dimensions."[44]

More recently, Stapp (1977), Kafatos and Nadeau (1990), Goswami et al. (1993) and Nesteruk (2000) have proposed that nonlocal processes involve a reality outside of space-time.[45] For Stapp (1977): "Everything we know about Nature is in accord with the idea that the fundamental process of Nature lies outside of space-time (surveys the space-time continuum globally), but generates events that can be located in space-time." Huston Smith, the prominent writer whose subject is world religions,[46] concluded (in a personal comment in 1997): "This makes that process metaphysical by including the physical while also being beyond and before it."

Propagated by the religions of all ages, categorically denied by the mechanistic sciences in the nineteenth century and their contemporary rearguard, the assumption of a transcendent part of reality is now possible and can serve as a basis of the human commitment to principles that transcend individual existence and needs. Teilhard had the courage to incorporate the transcendent world in his theory of evolution, regardless of whether or not it was scientifically acceptable.

3. Some Aspects of the Importance of Consciousness in the Physical World

Every mass is subject to the laws of relativity. Every system is quantized. But in slow-moving objects of ordinary size, relativistic and quantum effects are so subtle that they are not discoverable. That does not mean that they are not there. In objects moving at high velocities or in the elementary constituents of things, relativistic and quantum effects, respectively, clearly come to the fore.

The same pertains, Teilhard proposed, to effects of consciousness. In some things, there is no doubt that consciousness exists. It is clearly there. In others it also exists, but in such an attenuated state that it is not discoverable. Human beings clearly have a *within*. Elementary particles also have a within, even though it is so weakly expressed that it is not immediately visible. This is Teilhard's thesis of *"the Within of things"*;[47] it implies that an element of consciousness is active at all levels of reality.

> Coextensive with their Without, there is a Within to things.
> . . . Primitive matter is something more than the particulate
> swarming so marvelously analyzed by modern physics. Beneath
> the mechanical layer of primitive matter we must think of a bio-
> logical layer that is attenuated to the uttermost, but yet it is abso-
> lutely necessary to explain the cosmos in succeeding ages. The
> *within, consciousness* and then *spontaneity*—three expressions for the
> same thing.[48]

For these and similar passages, it is important to recall what Teilhard understood by "consciousness." It was not a symbolic or poetic term, but is taken in its widest sense to indicate every kind of psychicism, from the most rudimentary forms of interior perception imaginable to the human phenomenon of reflective thought.[49] The thesis that elements of consciousness are active at all levels of the universe is one of Teilhard's main themes. That consciousness may exist without a supporting material structure is a notion that science has always specifically denied, but may have to get used to. If we modify Teilhard's definition of "consciousness" by taking sensitivity to information as a sign of rudimentary consciousness, then we arrive indeed at the level of physical phenomena, confirming the view that all levels of reality are imbued with consciousness.

One must be quite clear about the fact that quantum theory cannot be taken as a license for proposing paranormal effects, esoteric new age theories and any form of magic. Nevertheless, one must take note that, at the level of elementary particles, aspects of consciousness appear in a rudimentary way in automatic, mechanical, and random reactions to the flow of information. Elementary particles thus differ from intelligent systems, which make use of information in a coordinated way for the purposes of their existence.

There is a hierarchy of intelligence in which systems with different degrees of freedom proceed from the vegetative level (as in plants and protozoa), to emerging forms of self-consciousness (as in domestic animals), and to higher levels of consciousness where human values, such as altruism, morality, and, finally, the understanding of abstract universal principles are effective factors. Beyond this hierarchy we can assume a level of consciousness that is not confined to space-time and not bound to localized material structures. Each higher level builds on the properties of the lower levels, without which it would not be possible. Without the mechanical consciousness of elementary particles and the automatic consciousness of the vegetative level, human consciousness would not be possible. One begins to suspect that none of these levels would be possible without the realm of nonmaterial transcendent consciousness. Thus, consciousness mirrors the quality of being real, which also forms a hierarchy of different levels, rising from a metaphysical basis through the quantum level, to the level of ordinary things. It is in agreement with the mind-like nature of the background of reality that "every time a richer and better organized structure will correspond to the more developed consciousness."[50]

The interactions of virtual (empty) states and actual (occupied) states offer a glimpse of how the mental can express itself in the material world. The first step lies in the transformation of a virtual state into an actualized state, transforming a virtual wave function to the wave function of a materially real state. Interestingly, both types of wave functions, virtual and materially real, are just invisible lists of numbers. They only differ in that the latter, *when probed*, can give rise to a real phenomenon, namely an observable probability distribution, while the former cannot be probed. Even the probability distributions are not individually visible but emerge only in repeated measurements made on an ensemble of the members of a given population. Thus the converting of mental (virtual) order to material (actual) order is possible because the first step is the subtle conversion among entities of the same kind—namely numbers.

The considerations above demonstrate that Teilhard's understanding of consciousness has found an exciting parallel in the quantum world. It is now possible to think that the mental element is the power of the universe. Logos, Mind, Nous, Weltgeist: By creating human minds it has found a new way to burst onto the scene. For Teilhard the consciousness of the world was the consciousness of the cosmic Christ. Thus he found, in a moving way, a synthesis of his scientific convictions and his religious faith. His vision of the science of the future gives reason for hope: "Like the meridians as they approach the poles, science, philosophy and religions are bound to converge as they draw nearer the whole."[51]

CHAPTER 9

The Role of Science in Contemporary China and according to Teilhard

Thierry Meynard, S.J.

For the past century, knowledge has been classified for the most part along Western lines in China. Thus, notions of science *(kexue)*, philosophy *(zhengzhi)*, and religion *(zongjiao)*, were neologisms introduced in China at the end of the nineteenth and beginning of the twentieth centuries. The introduction of these concepts (and here we especially concern ourselves with those of science and philosophy) oriented modern Chinese thought toward new debates that the Chinese had never experienced in the past. As modern Chinese thought derived its epistemology from the West, it should, by the same means, take in the different fields of inquiry underlying Western thought. Thus, the nineteenth-century European quarrel between scientific positivism and metaphysical philosophy would be reenacted in twentieth-century China in very similar terms.

Experts in Chinese studies will support the idea that Western scientific thought entered China through Jesuit missionary activities during the seventeenth and eighteenth centuries, notably in mathematics, astronomy, geography, medicine, and botany.

However, most of the Jesuits' knowledge was largely confined inside the walls of the imperial palace or the Astronomical Bureau in Beijing, and the Jesuits did not find Chinese institutions that would ensure the spread of this knowledge. At the beginning of the twentieth century, many research institutions were created on the model of those in the West, and in which Western institutions played an important role. When Teilhard de Chardin came to China, he first worked with the museum of natural history, founded by the Jesuit Emile Licent in Tianjin. Later on he worked as advisor to the *Geological Survey of China* founded in 1916. While the *Survey* was directed by the Chinese, many research programs were in fact directed by Western scientists, such as Amadeus W. Grabau, an American, and J. G. Anderson, a Swede. With the discovery of the Zhoukoudian site and its famous "Peking Man," the *Survey* collaborated with the Anatomy Department of the *American Hospital School* in Beijing, also called *Peking Union Medical College*. Davidson Black, an American, directed this unit, which benefited from the financial support of the Rockefeller Foundation. Teilhard worked within this research unit in the 1920s and '30s.

Modern science in China provoked a great fascination among many Chinese, especially for those who were now being trained by Western scientists in the new institutions mentioned above. However, it was traumatizing for many others, because this science seemed to make traditional Chinese thinking useless or even harmful. The schism created in the modern age in the West between science and metaphysics became more radicalized in twentieth-century China, because the debate was so central to Chinese cultural identity. This schism was clearly manifested during the dialectic over science and metaphysics which would stir up the Chinese intellectual world in the years 1923–24 and would determine to the present day the overarching direction of Chinese contemporary thought toward a type of scientism. The dialectic between science and metaphysics would explode during Teilhard's first stay in China. Within a period of a few months, some fifty articles would express the view of the greatest Chinese thinkers who would be divided amongst themselves between the metaphysical and scientific camps.

1. The Mutual Prejudices of the Metaphysicians and the Scientists

Zhang Junmai (1886–1969) began the debate in a conference in February 1923 at the University of Tsinghua. Zhang, like his contemporary neo-Confucians, sought scientific development because he recognized that knowledge for its own sake had not been sufficiently appreciated in China, and that it was important then to develop an epistemological spirit. He therefore did not oppose science, but he fiercely opposed scientism, which assumes that science is the only truth: "As developed as science can be, it cannot resolve the questions on the meaning of life because this is not within its power."[1] Zhang therefore came to describe the relationship between science and the meaning of human life through five major dichotomies: objectivity-subjectivity, logic-intuition, analysis-synthesis, causality-free will, and uniformity-diversity.

For Zhang, the cosmos is made up not only of the world of natural phenomena, but also of the world of metaphysical truth and morality. Scientific knowledge does not allow one to know the truth of things in itself, or the original essence of the world, because science based on the senses and reason remains a purely exterior knowledge. Only direct personal intuition of the mystical type allows a transcendence of the division between object and subject, and entry into a full knowledge that integrates the original eternal substance and its multiple phenomenal manifestations. Thus ultimately all knowledge is founded and accomplished in metaphysics. As for morality, the instrumental reason for science does not allow access to strictly ethical judgment. An objective scientific fact, which believes itself to be neutral and cut off from morality, ends in leading to a perverted morality, manipulating science with an eye toward utilitarian and hedonistic interests. It should be recognized therefore that even if the social sciences can adequately describe certain individual or social behaviors, they cannot claim to approach ethical questions, which remain outside the domain of science.

Zhang, and most neo-Confucians, share the conviction that modern Western culture has lost the balance between science and metaphysics. They emphasize the destruction of Western metaphysics, whose dogmatic affirmations have been contested by science, and criticize materialist Western civilization in that it threatens the essence of Chinese tradition, embodying as it does its own metaphysical and moral vision of the world and the cosmos. For them, the metaphysics of Chinese tradition not only does not contradict modern science, but should rectify the partial vision of scientism. In the background of the debate, one finds Zhang's judgments regarding the grave deficiencies of science. For him, science is responsible for the First World War, and the decline of civilization that resulted.

Zhang Junmai's vision of science contained certain simplifications which provoked a reaction from the scientist Ding Wenjiang (1887–1936), who attempted to correct the biases to which science falls victim. Ding, an eminent Chinese geologist, was the Director of the *Geological Survey of China* from its founding in 1916 until 1921. Teilhard would be his colleague a few years later. Ding attached himself to the school of logical positivism of Ernst Mach and the pragmatist school of John Dewey.[2] He contested Zhang's statements that science has nothing to say about the meaning of human life and defended the possibility that science can expand its competency from nature to society and the human spirit. Ding shared the same faith in science as those who belonged to the New Culture Movement *(Xinwenhua Yundong)*, which was started in 1919 by Chen Duxiu, Li Dazhao, Hu Shi, and others. They asserted that science and democracy are two references absolutely necessary to modern China. This faith in science came from nineteenth-century Europe, where the laws of science extended not only to the world of nature, but also to society and the economy. For Ding, the scientific laws, which would be revised in the future, permit a unity of human spirit and life, beyond the outdated particularities of culture. Moreover, Ding refuted the erroneous vision of matter and science proposed by Zhang Junmai. For Ding, matter is not inert but living. Further, science is not a completely objective exterior vision, but an activity internal to the human spirit, by which the spirit transforms and educates itself. Science is not a mechanical vision of reality. Finally, scientific activity, even if it relies on the concreteness of the physical world, does not become less of a spiritual activity than philosophy, and, like philosophy, science should be self-critical to achieve an authentic knowledge.

Ding's response not only serves to reestablish the contested power of science, but also to make science the unique means to a knowledge of reality. Faced with what Ding felt was a criticism of science by Zhang, who concluded that it was responsible for bringing about a materialist civilization and the disaster of the First World War, Ding responded by strengthening further his opposition to Zhang. Ding carried his attack to the heart of metaphysics. According to him, science refuted all metaphysics and made it an adversary, because, by scorning science, China turned back from the only road that could lead her toward progress. Also, evolution and materialism from then on rendered obsolete all metaphysics which claimed to erect eternal principles, because what evolution teaches us is that reality is a moving force, and what materialism teaches us is that reality is in fact a combination of forces. Thus the traditional metaphysics and the morality that ensues, be it Western or Confucian, no longer can face up to science. The only thing that matters is objective facts identified through science.

Ding came to adhere to "a scientific epistemology"; he believed that there could not be an epistemology other than one which rests solely on science, and it alone is capable of certainty, in contrast to philosophical idealism. He denied thus any other

means of knowledge. Clearly, Ding did not perceive the specific-
ity of philosophical knowledge and made scientific knowledge a
kind of determinism. A contemporary philosopher, Hu Shi, like
Ding a partisan of pragmatism, nevertheless realized: "Manifestly,
in mentioning his scientific epistemology, Ding committed an
error."[3] Ding also shared the faith of his age in the coming of
a superior humanity, which made him a promoter of a form of
eugenics.

The debate between science and metaphysics would finish with
the victory of science, rallying around it the greatest number of
voices. This victory of science in 1923 would, to a certain extent,
orient the principal current of Chinese thought in the twentieth
century. Nevertheless, the debate itself was the first indication of
a questioning of the power of science since its introduction into
China. The atrocities of the First World War had already shaken
a somewhat naïve optimism in science. With the debate sparked
by the metaphysicians on the subject of science, one witnesses the
first attempt to limit the impact and reach of this new triumphant
discipline.

If the questions of science are asked differently in China than
in the West, it is because the Chinese expect that science should
first resolve the question of survival of the nation, threatened by
those quasi-absolute possessors of modern science—the West.
The question of science in China takes on a particular political
importance in the context of a threatened nation. Ding is not only
a professional scientist, but also an important political player, having founded a weekly magazine, *Endeavor* (*Nuli*, 1922–23), in
which he affirmed that "politics is our only goal, reform our only
duty." The scientist owes it to himself to be a competent professional, but science is a political instrument, perhaps the most
powerful one, to protect the nation. To metaphysicians, who like
Zhang Junmai promoted traditional Chinese wisdom as a spiritual
gift, Ding responded that salvation for the Chinese comes first
through access to material riches, which is the only thing that will
permit the Chinese nation to hold a place on the international

scene. Teilhard would have been sorry to see this deep divide between science and metaphysics, while he himself tried to understand and to express their unity. However, China was bound to follow the even more radical stance of Marxist materialism.

2. The Impasse of Historical Materialism

During the twenties and thirties, the empirical scientism favored by liberals like Ding Wenjiang and Hu Shi made up the major current of scientism. Yet one result was that the materialist scientism favored by Chen Duxiu and the other Marxists became more influential. Contrary to empirical scientism, which considers science first as an epistemology, scientific materialism furnishes a complete explanation of all human reality and physics, which does not rely first on abstract notions of liberal idealism (man, nature of man), but rests on concrete "scientific" facts visible in social history. This materialist scientism differs from empirical scientism in that it is based on an underlying metaphysics. Indeed, even if Marxism rejects all metaphysical ontology, using as it does historical dialectics, it is still located nevertheless in the framework of an historical metaphysics, suggesting a vision of reality beyond the domain of empirical science. The scientific vulgate of Marxism radicalizes the view of empirical scientists, accused of not involving themselves in a complete materialism, which alone is capable of unifying nature and man, the natural sciences and the social sciences.

In Marxist scientism, individual liberty is undervalued, because even human conscience is in fact determined by one's social class. Humanity should recognize the existence of an objective world independent of human will, which obeys the laws of human development independent of will. Yet, humanity should lend its force to the anonymous powers of the works of history. At that level, it is no longer individual forces at work, but the collective forces that are strong enough to move history forward.

Chinese Marxist scientism is not a simple importation of outside thought. Materialist scientism maintains close bonds with a current of traditional Chinese culture that Hua Shiping defines as holistic, monist, or utopian. Without this deep cultural base, it is difficult to imagine how Marxist scientism succeeded in implanting itself in such a permanent manner in twentieth-century China.[4]

After the Cultural Revolution (1966–76), Deng Xiaoping prompted the modernization of four areas, science being the priority before the other three (industry, agriculture, and the army). At the moment of economic reform, science was again becoming the determining factor to raise productivity and get the economy back on track. At the same time, after the ideological divisions brought by the Cultural Revolution, it represented for society a neutral objective value upon which everyone could agree. Meanwhile science continued to play an ideological function for the elites who needed to legitimize their decisions. They felt that if they could not have scientific truth, a political truth that relied on science was essentially the same. One cannot help but ask oneself if this new form of scientism was sufficient to furnish an ideological base for political power.

Hu Shi wrote about this at the beginning of the twentieth century: "During the last thirty years, there is a name which has acquired an incomparable amount of respect. No one, be he well informed or ignorant, conservative or progressive, dares to openly scorn. This name is science."[5] It is an observation that is still valid today. As Hua Shiping notes, "Since the beginning of Chinese reforms (around 1890), there is no one in China who considers himself modern and who dares to openly put down science."[6] However, the attempts of Zhang Junmai and other neo-Confucians was intended precisely to circumscribe the area of science in order to free a necessary place for metaphysics. In fact, neither the scientists, nor the metaphysicians, nor Marxist philosophy succeeded in adequately articulating the two spheres of sciences and philosophy. Among the virulent scientific discussions that occupied all the intellectual space, a small band of intellectuals tried to intervene by emphasizing the preeminence of moral philosophy and metaphysics from which science can be deduced. Upon the statements of these intellectuals devaluing the methods and results of science, the scientists redoubled their efforts to eliminate what appeared to be the last vestiges of obscurantism. We remark that today we are still in large part divided between philosophy and science.

What was missing was an articulated connection that respected both the autonomy and intersection of the two spheres and ultimately presented a united non-totalitarian vision of the ensemble. Science is based on what the senses can apprehend, on experience. But the apprehension of reality is modeled on categories of thought, such as space, time, movement, energy: categories used in physics, but which are metaphysical concepts. Also science, without specializing in metaphysics, should recognize the metaphysical presuppositions that it employs. In another sense, philosophy does not restrict itself to the pure domain of ideas but recognizes the reality of phenomena. In this sense, what science unveils of the world is vital for science itself. Not only does philosophy disallow all affirmations that would contradict scientific knowledge, but, even more, it would seek to positively interpret and to extend scientific knowledge in exposing the meaning for humanity.

There are thinkers who have tried to surmount this dichotomy between science and philosophy. From the pair Zhang Junmai and Ding Wenjiang, I would like to move on to another pair in philosophy and science, Liang Shuming and Teilhard, to briefly describe here the efforts of these two men. The bringing together of Teilhard and Liang can be established through a simple historical fact: Both lived in Beijing and wrote their principal work there. *Human Spirit and Human Life*, was written by Liang in the 1950s and '60s, and *The Human Phenomenon* was written by Teilhard between 1938 and 1940. Both Liang and Teilhard attempted to bridge the gap between science and philosophy. Liang the philosopher included and interpreted scientific data into the spiritual development of human beings. Teilhard the scientist extended his scientific knowledge toward a philosophical investigation on the meaning of the human phenomenon.

3. *Liang Shuming: A Chinese Philosopher Bridging the Gap*

As we have seen, science presents a great challenge for the Chinese philosophical tradition, as well as for the West. The old metaphysics which underlies the Confucian morality needs to be reinterpreted in order to take on the challenge of science, not by denial, but by integrating the scientific vision of the world. Even modern Chinese metaphysics is challenged by science because it proposes a vision of the world based on an ultimate reality, which does not contradict the empirical facts of science, but interprets and integrates the results. Modern metaphysics could not regain its lost credibility by denigrating science, but in rearticulating its metaphysical intuitions on a creative interpretation of the world of nature. In the twentieth century, certain Chinese philosophers have tried to respond to this challenge by proposing a new epistemology that integrates science. Fang Dongmei (1899–1977) proposed a global vision of ascending evolution, while avoiding the traps that make nature sacred and a form of pantheism.[7]

Liang Shuming, a still more original thinker, incorporated certain aspects of the neo-Confucianism into a metaphysics that was essentially based on Buddhism. Liang was without a doubt one of the first in China to attempt to integrate the new vision of the world, as revealed by science, into traditional philosophy. Even if he maintained a certain duality between the scientific and ethical-spiritual approaches, attributing superiority to the latter, Liang, without being a scientist, was very interested in science. During the decade of 1910, he took seriously the discoveries of the structure of matter and tried to integrate them into the Buddhist phenomenology. Later, during the 1960s and '70s, he turned toward the natural sciences (natural history, biology, animal and human psychology, etc.) and tried to integrate them into Confucian metaphysics. In his last great work, *Human Spirit and Human Life*, finished in 1975 and published only in 1984, he undertook the task of describing the evolution of life, progressing in successive stages: instinct in the invertebrate kingdom, intelligence in the vertebrate kingdom, moral reason in man, union with the cosmos, and finally, ultimate projection into transcendence.

Liang accepts the evolutionist schema of Darwin and considers that life progresses in overcoming obstacles that it encounters. The animal world must resolve fundamental problems: survival of the species through biological reproduction and survival of individual members of the race. To resolve this double problem of life, the animal world, from protozoans to vertebrates, developed increasingly elaborate instincts. But in specializing itself to respond to environmental dangers, instincts isolate each animal species in its own narrow milieu. Now, for Liang, the direction of life is to go toward greater and wider communication with all things, toward a harmonious symbiosis among all the elements of nature based on a unity with a transcendent principle. Therefore, in enclosing itself in the problems of survival, each animal species comes to organize life in view of its particular survival and cuts itself off from the very direction of life, which is communication with everything.

The passage from invertebrate to vertebrate marks a radical change because, as the brain develops, invertebrate animals leave the domain of pure instinct, develop intelligence, and thereby create a greater distance between themselves and the immediate environment. Liang highlights the paradoxical character of this evolution, which culminates with human beings, because from the instinctual point of view this evolution marks a retreat relative to the invertebrates: The development of intelligence is accompanied by a diminution of instinctual capacities, making human beings the most vulnerable species. But for Liang, what we human beings lost in our capacity for immediate survival, for the species and for the individual, we gain by being able to enter into a larger and wider communion with the real nature of life, as we have distanced ourselves from the problem of survival which enclosed us in our instincts.

Through our intelligence, humans manage to objectify nature and to utilize our own abilities. But even when we control nature, we still remain a prisoner of necessity. It remains to us, therefore, to surmount this last obstacle by liberating ourselves from this law of necessity and so recover the original freedom of the moral life. Through self-perfection, in a Confucian tradition that goes from Mencius to Wang Yangming, Liang aims to develop or to uncover a nature, originally good and which manifests itself through a number of spontaneous moral sentiments (compassion, shame). In this way, human beings can recover the original state in which we can easily distinguish true from false, because we have turned away from all egocentric sentiment.

Socialization will continue to accompany the growth of humanity. If the first stages of society are marked by the necessity of mutual cooperation for the benefit of one and all, for Liang socialization marked an even more free and conscious choice, not dictated by necessity, but manifesting the real essence of life itself. Socialization pushes toward a more complete development of the human species. Morality is a free choice of humans, which manifests the real essence of life overcoming obstacles toward a greater communication with the universe.

The evolutionist schema of Liang rectifies several of Darwin's points. For example, he is in agreement with the Russian anarchist Pyotr Kropotkin (1842–1921) to affirm that evolution does not result from the struggle for life, but from mutual cooperation. However, he separates himself from Kropotkin on the fact that this mutual cooperation does not resort to an innate and mechanical instinct, but to morality aiming toward moral perfection.

The philosophical explanation by Liang of the human phenomenon is remarkable in several ways. First, while both Chinese and Western metaphysics often attributed a static place for human beings in nature, Liang takes into account the scientific theories of evolution of the species and of natural history, to refigure us as emerging and unfolding in nature. Secondly, the interpretation that Liang gave for life included intention, consciousness, judgment, and freedom as special functions of a natural process which are already present in the genesis of life. He felt that all of the facts identified and measured by the life sciences should be understood as an interpretation, not added on top of natural phenomena, but intrinsically tied in. Matter and spirit are not juxtaposed but they interpenetrate one another. Thirdly, the anthropo-cosmic vision of Liang leaves a large place for the progressive socialization of man, unifying in a synthetic vision natural sciences and social sciences. Fourth, Liang never goes into an easy pantheism that divinizes natural reality, but from his Buddhist faith, he maintains a radical transcendence which seeks itself in the cosmos, but extends beyond the cosmos.

4. Teilhard: A Western Scientist Bridging the Gap

Teilhard belongs to a long line of Jesuits who, for more than 450 years, have invested themselves in scientific research. If at certain times, the effort seems to have had a defensive motivation (to understand science in order to counter the challenge that it poses to faith), at the deepest level, the Jesuit scientists tried to show how scientific truths can still say something about God, even if they are incapable of demonstrating God. Teilhard devoted himself to the study of paleontology not only because it corresponded to his strongest personal interests, but also because this mission was given to him by the Jesuit order. During this period, at the start of the twentieth century, the Catholic Church and the Jesuits were in a defensive position with respect to evolutionist theory, and they decided to participate in these areas of research to challenge, on scientific grounds, the validity of certain theories. In

1914, Teilhard was thus sent by his superiors to do scientific research in paleontology, which was a decisive domain in the debate between the scientists and the religious faithful. At the price of a double fidelity to his faith and to scientific truth, Teilhard would try to reconcile the two.

While Teilhard's thought synthesized the physical world and the spiritual world, science and philosophy, it is important to remember what came from the scientific effort, and what from the philosophical effort. This ambiguity in Teilhard's thought made some people, such as Stephen Gould, unable to understand that the unitive vision of Teilhard is not situated in the same regime of truth as purely scientific affirmations. This unitive vision of reality is the extension of his scientific work, and at the same time, it is situated in another realm of truth. The two levels are not connected by a formal logical proof. Thus, the real difficulty for some scientists with Teilhard's thought is found where the distinction between the two levels is not sufficiently made clear, which already earned Teilhard the reproach from his professor, Marcellin Boule, for "his tendency to go beyond scientific fact to elevate himself to the level of a philosophical biologist."[8]

All scientific theories are based on metaphysical concepts, such as time, duration, space, etc. What verifies a scientific theory is not purely its formal logical coherence, but its agreement with observed facts. We can therefore say that the scientific theories of Teilhard are scientific in that they allow concrete phenomena to be made known. The difficulty with these theories is that they seem to assume too much, and that there is too much that escapes empirical verification. Yet since all scientific theories base themselves on metaphysical concepts, such as continuity or discontinuity of time, and continuity or discontinuity of space, they precede experience and are in themselves unverifiable. The scientists who refuse to recognize the metaphysical grounds of their discipline manifest in this way an irrational attitude. Teilhard calls science to come out of its too narrow limits: "In fact, science cannot reach the full limits of itself either in its impetus or in its constructions without being tinged with mysticism and charged with faith."[9] For Teilhard, this faith is double: faith in progress, as a conviction indemonstrable to science that the universe has a direction and it should arrive at its perfection, and faith in unity, like a partially supra-rational intuition of the convergence of the world.

Thus, the unity of the world does not spring from a scientific fact as such, but from an intuition, or vision, beyond empirical data. It is in this respect that Teilhard speaks about this unique science: "The further I go, the more I think the only science— that which one can acquire among all the weaknesses and ignorances—is the vision of unity in becoming—and by the incoherent multiplicity of things."[10] One can also consider the law of the growth of the unification of structures (growth of internal liaisons reinforcing the unity of the ensemble), to which Teilhard adheres, like a scientific hypothesis that asks to be judged by its coherence with scientific knowledge. This hypothesis is not contradicted by empirical facts held by the scientific world, and it also allows more intelligence to phenomena. If this criterion of coherence is respected, then we can hold this hypothesis as valid. It seems to me that we can reason in the same way with the other hypotheses of Teilhard. One such hypothesis would be the correspondence between external complexity and level of interiority— that is, the elevation of the level of consciousness proportional to the increase of connections with the outside. Another would be the dialectic of the continuity and discontinuity among the three levels of matter, life, and humanity—the passage to the next level through the accomplishment or maturation of the preceding level.

Since Teilhard is not content to describe the present or the past as fixed states, but tries to seize the phenomena in their genesis, he is led to reflect, as a scientist, about the future of the Earth and humanity. The scientific question of evolution, from the orientation of life, brings him to ask the philosophical question of meaning, of the finality of evolution. Darwin's schema of evolution is based first on the four causes of Aristotle, without presupposing any final cause and leaving room for chance. The final cause of the world, of life, does not spring from the strict domain of science, but from philosophy or theology. Teilhard observes these efficient and formal causes in the natural world and sees in them the signs of a final cause, but one that is not completely exterior to the actual process. It is a hypothesis that, for Teilhard, illuminates experience.

It could be observed that the Darwinian schema implies a kind of teleology, which puts human beings at the summit of a progressive evolution, as if it were making humans the goal of evolution. It is precisely this evolutionist schema that is contested by many people today. They feel that this anthropocentric vision, which makes human beings a species superior to the bee, should be rejected, since it is based on a value judgment without any scientific factual ground. Each species would be the result of different arrangements of nature, and all these different arrangements would hold the same value. If one arrangement develops into another, one could not nevertheless speak of progress. However, Teilhard succeeds in giving to human beings a unique place in the natural world, superior to the other species, but still insisting on his interrelatedness with nature. He provides an explanation of the teleology present in the Darwinian schema in maintaining a direction for evolution, as a progress toward consciousness. Teilhard affirms that there is a movement toward superior forms of consciousness. Human beings are the primordial point of this movement. We are nothing more than evolution being conscious of itself, nothing more than a consciousness capable of perceiving itself in the condensed simplicity of our faculties.

While science may see in this orientation merely a law endogenous to its own development, Teilhard saw something more: the design of a progress that leads toward an end. It is from this end, this final cause, which Teilhard called the omega point, that the world is being harmonized. All living beings are attracted toward the omega point. Science does not lead to Greek contemplation by which the spirit penetrates the immutable mysteries of the world. Nor does it lead to the Prometheism of modern science, which makes science the tool by which the human spirit is going to be able to dominate nature. For Teilhard, science was first the effort of the human spirit seizing upon its own drive to work in nature. It is therefore science that finally allows humanity to accompany evolution, even to the point of directing it; science is not perceived as a simple tool, but something that Teilhard places at the summit of human consciousness.

While it is common for scientists to specialize, Teilhard demonstrated a science capable of synthesis beyond strict academic divisions. He criticized the modern science that revolves around analysis, and neglects the synthesis that would permit it to see the independence and the stability of what emerges beyond isolated elements. Teilhard, who was highly qualified in geology, paleontology, and anthropology, could see the same movement of life at work everywhere. In geology, he perceived the geological layers of the earth as an immense living organism. In paleontology, he demonstrated that species evolve not only by breakthroughs but also in parallel. In anthropology, he studied the lengthy development of hominization. In these three domains, Teilhard saw a unique movement associating matter and the living, lithosphere and biosphere, which he called geobiology. Matter, life, and spirit are interdependent. Matter irradiates interiority and intelligence. Human reflection is not a simple addendum to the evolutionary process, but something that emerges from the process itself. Thus physics and the psyche are tied in the same process. There exists a profound union between the material and the spiritual: unity of reality in a logical and coherent structure (at the risk of rationalism sometimes, devaluing the concrete and individual existence of beings and attenuating the discontinuities). The progress of consciousness and the progress of material organization don't simply accompany one another, but are two sides of the same phenomenon. Matter is only the tangible appearance of energy. Now, for Teilhard, the term energy is different from that of a physicist, because Teilhard goes so far as to speak of spiritual energy, with the problem of quantifying it, and also to postulate a finality, an actor above phenomena. This affirmation, while being extra-scientific, does not deny scientific fact, but gives them a greater coherence of thought. The notion of spiritual energy is not mechanical causality, since it integrates the determinisms without destroying them, and it gives a philosophical interpretation to the historical fact of thought.

5. The Agreements and Differences between Teilhard and Liang Shuming

Teilhard the scientist and Liang the philosopher maintained very similar positions. For both the world was based on freedom. Physiological determinations do not so much limit our freedom, as reveal more profoundly the results of our moral choices. Both saw the world of invertebrates as an impasse. The insects got into this impasse because of their psychological inferiority: Their consciousness is extroverted in the mechanical and rigid movements of instinct. Even if the nervous system can develop in mammals, they have become imprisoned by the accessory specializations that limit them. Dimmed by their drive for survival, the members of the species try to individualize themselves, to differentiate themselves, and by doing so, they cut themselves off from the movement of life which is driven toward unification. Thus, it is possible to apply moral categories to life forms, like freedom or egotism. Teilhard speaks of this egotism in the work of nature: "Its only mistake, but a fatal one that leads it to go astray, is to confuse *individuality with personality*. In trying to distinguish itself as much as possible from others, the element individualizes itself; but in doing so it falls back and tries to drag the world backward toward plurality and into matter. In reality, the element diminishes itself and becomes lost. To become fully ourselves, it is in the opposite direction we must advance, in the direction of convergence with all the rest, toward the 'other.'"[11] As a result of egoism, the species stops in evolution or perhaps even regresses to the point of proving incapable of adapting to new conditions of life and so disappears completely. For the egocentric, the ideal future is reserved for those who know how to arrive at the extreme of each one for oneself: a position which is false and unnatural. No element can move or become greater without the other elements. For both Liang and Teilhard, the great lesson of life is to always progress toward greater communion. Both of them see a fundamental moral law which structures life itself. Life is communion—communion of the multitude of beings among each other and with the whole. Teilhard thus describes the noosphere: It "is tending to make up a single closed system in which each element sees, feels, desires, and suffers for itself the same things at the same time as all the others; a harmonized collectivity of consciousness, equivalent to a kind of superconsciousness."[12] Thus the fulfillment of life is to surpass the limits of individuality, to merge with the cosmos by the tightest interplay of interdependences. This growth of the consciousness of interdependence leads then to a "generalized ultra-responsibility."

The second common feature is that both Teilhard and Liang recognized the forces for survival at work in cells, individuals, and species, as in societies. But both emphasized that progress consists of going beyond the primary destructive fight in the direction of solidarity, interdependence, symbiosis, life in community, and association. The direction of evolution is really this surmounting of division toward a greater unity, because as Teilhard says: "Insofar as the general movement of life becomes more ordered, in spite of periodic resumptions of the offensive the conflicts tend to resolve themselves. Yet it is cruelly recognizable right to the end. Only from the spirit, where it reaches its *felt* paroxysm, will the antinomy clear; and the world's indifference to its element be transformed into an immense solicitude—in the sphere of the person."[13]

Finally, the anthropo-cosmic vision of Teilhard and Liang are remarkable in that they never fall into an easy pantheism. On the contrary, Liang, in his Buddhist faith, maintains an exit from the history of the world, toward a radical transcendence. Teilhard, in the same way, in his Christian faith, maintains that the world is headed toward the point of ultimate transcendence which he calls omega. For Teilhard, the noosphere, the last stage of evolution, is based on God-Omega. The end of the world is seen as "the noosphere's internal turning back on itself as a unit, having simultaneously reached its utmost degree of complexity and concentration . . . the reversal of equilibrium, detaching the spirit, complete at last, from its material matrix, to rest from now on with its whole weight on God-Omega."[14] The four attributes of the omega, as Teilhard describes them, are autonomy, currency, irreversibility, and transcendence.

Even if the emphasis here has been the points of agreement between Teilhard and Liang, nonetheless their attitude in relation to the world was profoundly different. For Liang, raised in a Confucian and Buddhist culture, as human beings we unite ourselves to the movement of life and the cosmos, but we can't do it truthfully except at the price of a certain detachment from the material world. Confucianism teaches that moral perfection is acquired by becoming free of the excessive hold on earthly desires. Buddhism teaches in a more radical manner the actual extinction of all desires. The Confucian asceticism and the piercing consciousness of suffering in Buddhism are necessary stages toward purification of the spirit. For Teilhard, it is this question of attitude to the world where the East and the West diverge. If Teilhard admires Chinese thought for its sympathy toward humanity, he judges that it does not go far enough in its faith in humanity nor does it encourage engagement in the world:

> Thus the East fascinates me by its faith in the final unity of the universe. But it turns out that we have, the East and myself, two opposing conceptions about the relations in the passage between

totality and its elements. For them, the One appears out of suppression and for me, it is born from the concentration of the multiple . . . China is, and has been for a long time, a crucible par excellence of material and human aspirations. What characterizes its soul is its interest in man, more certainly than its faith in man.[15]

Conclusion

Both in the West and in China, the twentieth century has experienced a harsh opposition between science and metaphysics, between materialism and idealism. Therefore it is astonishing to see these two men, Teilhard de Chardin and Liang Shuming, who didn't know each other and who came from such different intellectual traditions, arrive at such similar visions, and who wrote their major books in Beijing almost at the same time. Both of them had fully accepted the fact of evolution at work in the natural world and had extended it into the humane world. They have successfully integrated the world of nature and the world of human beings into a moral law of consciousness inscribed inside the very process or unfolding of reality. They have envisioned the future of a humanity attaining a completely new stage of interdependence and unity, even though expressed in two different models—the Church for Teilhard, and the socialist society for Liang. Finally, they have held that the rise of consciousness in the world could achieve its unfolding only in a radical transcendence.

Translated by Tracy Higgins

NOTES

FEEDING THE ZEST FOR LIFE:
SPIRITUAL ENERGY RESOURCES FOR THE FUTURE OF HUMANITY
Ursula King

1. Teilhard de Chardin, *The Future of Man*, trans. Norman Denny (London: Collins, 1964), 7.

2. Teilhard de Chardin, *The Human Phenomenon*, trans. Sarah Appleton-Weber (Brighton and Portland: Sussex Academic Press, 1999).

3. I have discussed these in detail in my essay, "Teilhard's Association with the World Congress of Faiths, 1947–50" in Ursula King, *The Spirit of One Earth: Reflections on Teilhard de Chardin and Global Spirituality* (New York: Paragon House, 1989), 135–46; see also chap. 4 in my book *Towards a New Mysticism: Teilhard de Chardin and Eastern Religions* (London: Collins; New York: Seabury Press, 1980).

4. Teilhard de Chardin, *The Future of Man*, 185–92.

5. Ibid., 190.

6. Ibid., 193–95.

7. Ibid., 194.

8. See Teilhard de Chardin, *Activation of Energy* (London: Collins, 1970), 229–43.

9. Ibid., 231–32.

10. Howard Thurman, *Meditations of the Heart* (Boston: Beacon Press, 1981), 134.

11. *The Human Phenomenon*, 161.

12. Eduard Suess, *The Face of the Earth*, 5 vols. (Oxford: Clarendon Press, 1904–24). Popular as a textbook in geology for many years, this is a translation of his work *Das Antlitz der Erde*, published 1883–1901.

157

13. See "La face de la terre," *Études* 169 (1921): 585–602; translated as "The Face of the Earth," in Teilhard de Chardin, *The Vision of the Past* (London: Collins, 1966), 26–48. The quotation given here forms part of an excerpt of this essay reproduced in a somewhat different translation in Teilhard de Chardin, *Hymn of the Universe* (London: Collins Fount Paperbacks 1986), 75; the text in *The Vision of the Past* is slightly different.

14. See his article "The Formation of the Noosphere: A Biological Interpretation of Human History," in *The Future of Man*, 155–84.

15. Paul R. Samson and David Pitt, eds., *The Biosphere and Noosphere Reader: Global Environment, Society and Change* (London and New York: Routledge, 1999).

16. Ibid., 181.

17. Ibid., 186.

18. Published in his book *Human Energy* (London: Collins, 1969), 19–47.

19. Ibid., quotation at 19, note 1.

20. Ibid., quotations at 27–29, 31, 37.

21. Ibid., 35.

22. Ibid., 31.

23. Ibid., 32.

24. Ibid., 33–34.

25. Ibid., 35 (my translation).

26. The French original reads "l'amour d'interliaison, au-dessus de l'amour d'attrait." See *L'énergie humaine*, vol. 6 of *Oeuvres*, 44.

27. Ibid., 38.

28. This as well as the previous quotations are from *L'energie humaine*, 37f.

29. Ibid.

30. *Human Energy*, 44.

31. Teilhard de Chardin, *Man's Place in Nature* (London: Collins, 1966), 118.

32. Ibid.

33. Found in the book of the same title; see *Human Energy*, 113–62.

34. *Activation of Energy*, 236.

35. Ibid., 238.

36. Ibid., 241. A fuller discussion of this is found in King, *Towards a New Mysticism: Teilhard de Chardin and Eastern Religions.*

37. *Activation of Energy*, 242. I have discussed Teilhard's understanding of love in my article "Love—A Higher Form of Human Energy in the Work of Teilhard de Chardin and Sorokin," in *Zygon: Journal of Religion and Science* 39, no. 1 (2004): 77–102.

38. Thomas Berry, *The Great Work: Our Way into the Future* (New York: Bell Tower, 1999).

39. Robert Muller, *New Genesis: Shaping a Global Spirituality* (New York: Doubleday, 1982).

40. *The Human Phenomenon*, 161.

GOD AND THE HUMAN FUTURE
Thomas M. King, S.J.

1. Teilhard de Chardin, *Writings in Time of War* (New York: Harper and Row, 1968), 179.

2. Teilhard de Chardin, *The Heart of Matter*, trans. René Hague (New York: Harcourt Brace Jovanovich, 1979), 176–77.

3. Ibid., 178.

4. Ibid., 173.

5. Ibid., 179; see also *Writings in Time of War*, 291.

6. Ibid., 176.

7. Teilhard de Chardin, *The Phenomenon of Man*, trans. Bernard Wall (New York: Harper and Row, 1959), 110.

8. Teilhard de Chardin, *Writings in Time of War*, 231.

9. Teilhard de Chardin, *The Heart of Matter*, 176.

10. Ibid., 178.

11. Teilhard de Chardin, *The Phenomenon of Man*, 251, 246.

12. Ibid., 269.

13. Teilhard de Chardin, *Christianity and Evolution*, trans. René Hague (New York: Harcourt Brace Jovanovich, 1971), 124.

14. Teilhard de Chardin, *Human Energy*, trans. J. M. Cohen (New York: Harcourt Brace Jovanovich, 1969), 147.

15. Ibid., 148.

16. Ibid., 47.

17. Teilhard de Chardin, *The Divine Milieu* (New York: Harper and Row, 1960), 65.

18. Ibid., 65, 70.

19. "Les miracles de Lourdes et les enquêtes canoniques," in *Etudes* (January 1909): 182.

20. Teilhard de Chardin, *Christianity and Evolution*, 28–29.

21. Teilhard de Chardin, *The Phenomenon of Man*, 233.

22. Ibid., 275–76.

23. Unpublished Journal of Teilhard de Chardin, March 23, 1922; these are available in the Georgetown University Library.

24. Letter (unpublished), Teilhard de Chardin to Abbé Breuil, July 25, 1923; available at Georgetown University Library.

25. Pierre Teilhard de Chardin, *Letters from a Traveler* (New York and Evanston: Harper and Row, 1962), 33.

26. Josef Pieper, *Leisure: The Basis of Culture*, trans. Gerald Malsbary (South Bend: St. Augustine's Press, 1998), 68.

1. Teilhard de Chardin, *Le cœur de la matière*, vol. 13 of *Oeuvres*, 45.

2. Ibid., 40–41.

3. Ibid., 41–42.

4. Ibid. *Le cœur de la matière* ends with a part called "Le féminin ou l'unitif," 71–75.

5. Teilhard de Chardin, "Esquisse d'un univers personnel," dated Beijing, 1936, (unpublished).

6. "Le phénomène humain," *Revue des questions scientifiques* (Novembre 1930); included in *La vision du passé*, vol. 3 of *Oeuvres*, 227–44.

7. Ibid., 241.

8. Conference given in Beijing on November 15, 1942; published in *Être plus* (Paris: Editions Le Seuil, 1968).

9. "Le phénomène humain," *Revue des questions scientifiques;* also in *La vision du passé*, vol. 3 of *Oeuvres*, 241.

10. "La grande option," *Cahiers du Monde nouveau* 1, no. 3 (1945); included in *L'avenir de l'homme*, vol. 5 of *Oeuvres*, 73–74.

11. Teilhard, *Le phénomène humain*, 22.

12. Teilhard de Chardin, "La grande option," in *L'avenir de l'homme*, vol. 5 of *Oeuvres*, 78–79.

13. Henri de Lubac, *La pensée religieuse du Père Pierre Teilhard de Chardin* (Editions Aubier, 1962); new ed. (Editions du Cerf, 2002), 204.

14. Ibid., 149–50.

15. Teilhard de Chardin, "L'esprit de la terre," in *L'activation de l'energie*, vol. 7 of *Oeuvres*.

16. Teilhard de Chardin, "Sur les bases possibles d'un Credo humain," in *L'avenir de l'homme*, vol. 5 of *Oeuvres*, 103.

17. Cf: Teilhard de Chardin, "Comment je vois," in *Les directions de l'avenir*, vol. 11 of *Oeuvres*; "La Centrologie," in *L'activation de l'energie*, vol. 7 of *Oeuvres*; "Le Rebondissement humain de l'evolution," in *L'avenir de l'homme*, vol. 5 of *Oeuvres*; "Montée irrésistible vers le Personnel," 265.

18. Henri de Lubac, 150; Teilhard de Chardin, "Les directions et les conditions de l'avenir," in *L'avenir de l'homme*, vol. 5 of *Oeuvres*, 305.

ZEST FOR LIFE: TEILHARD'S COSMOLOGICAL VISION
Mary Evelyn Tucker

1. See the series of articles that were published over the last 25 years by the American Teilhard Association exploring Teilhard's cosmological vision in Arthur Fabel and Donald St. John, eds., *Teilhard in the Twenty-First Century: The Emerging Spirit of the Earth* (Maryknoll, New York: Orbis Books, 2003).

2. Teilhard, *Human Energy* (London: Collins, 1969), 51.

3. This is the perspective that has been richly developed by Thomas Berry in *The Dream of the Earth* (Sierra Club Books, 1988) and by Brian Swimme and Thomas Berry in *The Universe Story* (Harper: San Francisco, 1992).

4. Teilhard de Chardin, *Human Energy*, 82.

5. Teilhard de Chardin, *The Human Phenomenon*, 24.

6. Teilhard de Chardin, *Science and Christ*, trans. René Hague (London: Collins and New York: Harcourt Brace Jovanovich, 1968), 193.

7. Mihaly Csikszentmihalyi, *The Evolving Self* (New York: Harper Collins, 1993), 19.

8. Ibid., 25.

9. Teilhard de Chardin, *The Future of Man*, 118.

TEILHARD'S VISION AND THE EARTH CHARTER
Steven C. Rockefeller

1. Teilhard de Chardin, *The Phenomenon of Man*, trans. Bernard Wall (New York: Harper, 1959), 239.

2. Ibid., 181–83, 212, 215, 221, 239, 258.

3. Ibid., 222, 234, 242–43, 284–85.

4. Ibid., 244–46, 253, 264–66. See also Teilhard de Chardin, "The Spirit of Earth," in *Building the Earth*, trans. Noël Linsay (Paris: Editions du Seuil, 1958). In the English translations of Teilhard's works, sometimes the word "earth" is not capitalized, as in *The Phenomenon of Man*, and in other instances it is capitalized as in the essay "The Spirit of Earth." In "The Spirit of Earth" sometimes the definite article is used and sometimes it is not. The Earth Charter uses the name "Earth," which is common practice among astronomers and many other scientists. Using "Earth" rather than "the earth" evokes the awesome image of the planet in space as photographed by the astronauts whereas references to "the earth" can reinforce the problematic tendency in modern society to think of the planet as merely an object that exists solely for human use and exploitation. The new global ethics affirms respect for Earth and the greater community of life in all its diversity as a fundamental principle. This principle is supported by Teilhard's world view.

5. See Earth Charter, Preamble.

6. Aldo Leopold, *A Sand County Almanac* (New York: Ballantine Books, 1970), 238–39.

7. For the text of the Earth Charter and more information on the Earth Charter Initiative, see the international Earth Charter secretariat website www.earthcharter.org.

8. Teilhard de Chardin, *Activation of Energy*, trans. René Hague (New York: Harcourt Brace, 1971), 171–79, 209, 284.

9. Even though the concept of sustainable development was constructed several decades after Teilhard's career ended, he would surely have actively supported it as an ecological and social ideal had he lived to see its emergence. Sustainability is implicit in his concept of a love that "embraces the total of man and of the earth."

10. UN Millennium Declaration, I. Values and Principles. #6. Respect for Nature.

11. World Commission on Environment and Development, *Our Common Future* (New York: Oxford, 1987), 57.

12. The Johannesburg Declaration on Sustainable Development states: "From this continent, the cradle of humanity, we declare, through the Plan of Implementation of the World Summit on Sustainable Development and the present Declaration, our responsibility to one another, to the greater community of life and to our children" (paragraph 6). For the complete text, see http://www.un.org/esa/sustdev/documents/Johannesburg%20Declaration.doc.

13. Teilhard de Chardin, "The Evolution of Responsibility in the World," in *Activation of Energy*, 207–14. Teilhard de Chardin, "The Spirit of Earth."

14. Information on this project can be found at http://www.earthcat.org.

15. For more information on the Decade of Education for Sustainable Development, see the UNESCO website: http://portal.unesco.org/education/en/ev.php-URL_ID = 23279&URL_DO = DO_TOPIC&URL_SECTION = 201.html.

TEILHARD, GLOBALIZATION AND THE
FUTURE OF HUMANITY
Michel Camdessus

1. Teilhard de Chardin, *Le milieu divin*, vol. 4 of *Oeuvres*, 65.

2. Ibid., 74.

3. Conference given in Beijing on December 28, 1943; *Réflexions sur le bonheur*, in *Les directions de l'avenir*, vol. 11 of *Oeuvres*.

4. Ephesians 1:10.

5. Romans 8:20–21.

6. Journal, 7 April 1955.

7. Journal, 7 April 1955; On 9 March 1952, he wrote also: "Is not the greatest joy to be found in having perceived that the World has a Center, and that this Center is loving?"

8. Teilhard de Chardin, *Science et Christ*, vol. 9 in *Oeuvres*, 259.

9. Jean-Baptiste De Foucauld, *Les trois cultures du développement humain* (Paris: Editions Odile Jacob, 2002).

10. Cf. Jean-Luc Domenach, "Un monde peu teilhardien?" in *Avec Pierre Teilhard de Chardin, 2003 Pékin, Science et progrès humain* (Paris: Aubin, 2004), 217–22.

11. John Paul II, *Sollicitudo Rei Socialis* 17, *AAS* 80 (1988): 532.

12. Teilhard de Chardin, *Lettres à l'abbé Gaudefroy et à l'abbé Breuil* in *Lettres inédites 1923–1955* (Monaco: Editions du Rocher, 1988).

13. The Millennium Development Goals (MDG) are to, by 2015,
    1. diminish by half the proportion of those persons living in extreme poverty, those suffering from hunger, and those who do not have access to potable water;
    2. put in place universal primary education and obtain the equality of the sexes in education;
    3. reduce by three-fourths maternal mortality and by two-thirds infant mortality for those under the age of five;
    4. stop the progression of the HIV/AIDS epidemic and start to reduce it;
    5. ameliorate the lives of 100 million persons living in slums.

14. Teilhard to Claude Aragonnés, 2 May 1917, in *Genèse d'une pensée: Lettres à Claude Aragonnés* (Paris: B. Grasset, 1961), 232.

15. http://www.imf.org/external/am/2000/speeches/PR01F.pdf.

16. Ibid.

17. Teilhard de Chardin, *L'avenir de l'homme*, vol. 5 of *Oeuvres*, 365–74, quotation at Bernard Sesé, *Études* (2002): 3964.

18. R. M. Rilke, quotation at J. Mambrino, *La Pénombre de l'Or* (Paris: Arfuyen, 2002).

TEILHARD AND GLOBALIZATION
Jean Boissonnat

1. Teilhard de Chardin, *Le milieu divin*, vol. 4 of *Oeuvres*, 50.

2. Pierre Léon, *L'ouverture du monde XIVe–XVIe siècles* (Editions Armand Colin, 1977), 578.

3. Angus Maddison, *World Economy: A Millennial Perspective* (Paris: Development Centre of the Organisation for Economic Co-operation and Development, 2001).

4. David S. Landes, *Richesse et pauvreté des nations* (Paris: Editions Albin Michel, 2000).

5. Pope John Paul II, *Laborem Exercens*, 1981.

6. Pope John Paul II, *Centesimus Annus*, 1991.

7. Quoted by Angus Maddison in *World Economy*.

8. *Population et société* (September 2000).

9. *Le cœur de la matière*, vol. 13 of *Oeuvres*.

10. Lecture given at Paris in January 2001, available at *Documentation Catholique*, www.doc-catho.com.

THE EMERGENCE OF CONSCIOUSNESS IN BIOLOGICAL EVOLUTION
AND QUANTUM REALITY
Lothar Schäfer

1. St Augustine, *Confessions* (*Augustinus Bekenntnisse*, Reclam, 1989), 169.

2. J. S. Bell, "On the Einstein Podolsky Rosen Paradox," *Physics* 1 (1965): 195–200; J. S. Bell, Interview, *Omni* 10, no. 8 (1988): 84–121; A. Aspect, P. Grangier, G. Roger, *Physical Review Letters*, 47 (1981): 460; A. Aspect, J. Dalibart, and R. Roger, *Physical Review Letters* 49 (1982): 1804; B. d'Espagnat, *Physical Review Letters* 49 (1981): 1804; A. Shimony, *Physics Today* 44 (August 1991): 82–86.

3. John Polkinghorne, *Belief in God in an Age of Science* (New Haven: Yale University Press, 1998), 66.

4. John Archibald Wheeler and Kenneth Ford, *Geons, Black Holes and Quantum Foam* (New York: Norton, 1998), 340.

5. H. P. Stapp, "Are Superluminal Connections Necessary?" *Nuovo Cimento* 40B (1977): 191–99.

6. Norbert Wiener, *Cybernetics* (New York: MIT Press, 1961), 132.

7. A. S. Eddington, *The Nature of the Physical World* (New York: Macmillan, 1929), 276; *The Philosophy of Physical Science* (New York: Macmillan, 1939), 151.

8. James Jeans, *The Mysterious Universe* (New York: Macmillan, 1931), 146, 158.

9. Henry Margenau, *The Miracle of Existence* (Woodbridge, CT: Ox Bow Press, 1984), 16.

10. A. S. Eddington, *The Nature of the Physical World* (New York: Macmillan, 1929), 309.

11. Kenneth R. Miller, *Finding Darwin's God* (New York: Cliff Street Books, 1999), 190.

12. Ibid., 168.

13. Werner Heisenberg, "Ideas of the Natural Philosophy of Ancient Times in Modern Physics" in *Philosophical Problems of Quantum Physics* (Woodbridge, Conn.: Ox Bow Press, 1952); *Physics and Philosophy* (New York: Harper Torchbook, 1962).

14. Teilhard de Chardin, *La place de l'homme dans la nature*, vol. 8 of *Oeuvres*, 50.

15. Teilhard de Chardin, *The Phenomenon of Man*, trans. Bernard Wall (New York: Harper and Row, 1959), 30.

16. Jacques Monod, *Chance and Necessity* (London: Collins, 1972), 113.

17. Lothar Schäfer, "On the Halfway Reductionism of Michael Ruse," in *Research News and Opportunity in Science and Theology* 2, no. 4 (December 2001): 16; "Quantum View of Evolution" in *Research News and Opportunity in Science and Theology* 2, no. 8 (April 2002): 26; "Biology Must Consider Quantum Effects" in *Research News and Opportunity in Science and Theology* 3, no. 1 (September 2002): 16; "*Versteckte Wirklichkeit—Wie uns die Quantenphysik zur Transzendenz führt*" (Stuttgart: Hirzel, 2004).

18. C. Van Alsenoy, C.-H. Yu, A. Peeters, J. M. L. Martin, L. Schäfer, "Ab Initio Geometry Determination of Proteins. I. Crambin" in *Journal of Physical Chemistry* 102 (1998): 2246–51; X. Jiang,

M. Cao, B. Teppen, S. Q. Newton, and L. Schäfer, "Predictions of Protein Backbone Structural Parameters from First Principles: Systematic Comparisons of Calculated N-C(α)-C', Angles with High-Resolution Protein Crystallographic Results," *Journal of Physical Chemistry* 99 (1995): 10521; L. Schäfer, C. Van Alsenoy, and J. N. Scarsdale, "Ab Initio Studies of Structural Features not Easily Amenable to Experiment, 23. Molecular Structures and Conformational Analysis of the Dipeptide N-acetyl-N'-methyl glycyl amide and the Significance of Local Geometries for Peptide Structures," *Journal of Physical Chemistry* 76 (1982): 1439.

19. See, e.g. B. J. Teppen, C.-H. Yu, S. Q. Newton, D. M. Miller, and L. Schäfer, "Quantum Molecular Dynamics Simulations Regarding the Dechlorination of Trichloro Ethene in the Interlayer Space of the 2:1 Clay Mineral Nontronite," *Journal of Physical Chemistry* 106 (2002): 5498–503.

20. F. Millett, and B. Durham, "Design of Photoactive Ruthenium Complexes to Study Interprotein Electron Transfer," *Biochemistry* 41 (2002): 11315–24.

21. For a summary see Lee M. Spetner, *Not by Chance! Shattering the Modern Theory of Evolution* (New York: Judaica Press, 1997).

22. Teilhard de Chardin, *The Phenomenon of Man*, 121.

23. J. S. Gould, and N. Eldredge, "Punctuated Equilibrium Comes of Age," *Nature* 366 (1993): 223–27; N. Eldredge and S. J. Gould, in *Models of Palaeobiology*, ed. Thomas J. M. Schopf (San Francisco: Freeman, Cooper, 1972), 82–115.

24. J. D. Ewbank, L. Schäfer, and A. A. J. Ischenko, *Journal of Molecular Structure* 321 (1994): 265–78.

25. Ibid.

26. Ibid.

27. Michael Ruse, and E. O. Wilson, "The Approach of Sociobiology: The Evolution of Ethics" in James E. Huchingson, ed., *Religion and the Natural Sciences* (New York: Harcourt, Brace, Jovanovich, 1993), 310.

28. M. Ruse, "The Bad Smell of Anti-reductionism," *Research News and Opportunity in Science and Theology* 1, no. 9 (May 2001): 27.

29. Ursula King, *Spirit of Fire* (New York: Orbis Books Maryk-noll, 1996); M. Trennert-Hellwig, *Die Urkraft des Kosmos* (Freiburg: Herder, 1993).

30. Teilhard de Chardin, *La place de l'homme dans la nature*, vol. 8 in *Oeuvres*, 34.

31. Teilhard de Chardin, *The Heart of Matter*, 25.

32. Teilhard de Chardin, *La place de l'homme dans la nature*, 35, 44.

33. Teilhard de Chardin, *The Phenomenon of Man*, 57.

34. Ibid., 54–57.

35. Teilhard de Chardin, "Mon univers," in *Science et Christ*, vol. 9 in *Oeuvres*, 74.

36. Teilhard de Chardin, *The Phenomenon of Man*, 30.

37. Ibid., 153.

38. Ibid., 165.

39. Teilhard de Chardin, *La place de l'homme dans la nature*, 153.

40. Teilhard de Chardin, *The Phenomenon of Man*, 225.

41. Ibid., 226–29.

42. Teilhard de Chardin, *La place de l'homme dans la nature*, 165–67.

43. Ibid., 172.

44. James Jeans, *The Mysterious Universe*, 132.

45. Amit Goswami, Richard E. Reed, and Maggie Goswami, *The Self-Aware Universe* (New York: Penguin Putnam, 1993); Menas Kafatos and Robert Nadeau, *The Conscious Universe* (New York: Springer Verlag, 1990); A. V. Nesteruk, "Is a Wave Function Collapse a Real Event in Physical Space and Time?" in *Material Interpretations*, ed. M. C. Duffy and M. Wegener, vol. 2 of *Recent Advances in Relativity Theory* (Palm Harbor, Fla.: Hadronic Press, 2000), 169–170; H. P. Stapp, "Are Superluminal Connections Necessary?" in *Nuovo Cimento* 40B (1977): 191–99.

46. Huston Smith, *The Religions of Man* (New York: Harper, 1958).

47. Teilhard de Chardin, *The Phenomenon of Man*, 54–57.

48. Teilhard de Chardin, *The Phenomenon of Man*, 56.

49. Ibid., 57.

50. Ibid., 60.

51. Ibid., 30.

THE ROLE OF SCIENCE IN CONTEMPORARY CHINA AND
ACCORDING TO TEILHARD
Thierry Meynard, S.J.

1. Zhang Junmai, *Rensheng Guan* (The vision of human life) (Beijing: Zhongguo Guangbodianshe, 1995), 7.

2. Mach's school of logical positivism was based in Vienna and spread mostly through the German-speaking regions. It affirmed that a truth is only scientific when this truth can be verified. Everything which does not flow logically from facts is only metaphysics and, therefore for this school, an absurdity. For John Dewey and the school of pragmatism, the truth or the value of a theory or hypothesis depends on its positive results. What is scientific is none other than an appellation a posteriori for what has undergone testing and which yields practical results.

3. Hu Shi, *Biography of Ding Wenjiang (Ding Wenjiang Zhuan)* (Hainan: Hainan Chubanshe, 1993), 118.

4. Cf. Shiping Hua, *Scientism and Humanism* (State University of New York Press), 16.

5. Ibid., 145.

6. Ibid.

7. Zhang Chunshen, *A Life Christology (Shengming Jidulun)* in *Collectanea Theologica Universitatis Furen*, 112 (Summer 1997): 171–78. The philosophy of Fang Dongmei, like Teilhard's, is not a pantheism but a pan-en-theism, since the world is included in God, but God is more than the world.

8. Louis Baron and Pierre Leroy, *La Carrière Scientifique de Pierre Teilhard de Chardin* (Monaco: Editions du Rocher, 1964), 21.

9. *The Human Phenomenon* (Brighton: Sussex Academic Press, 1999), 203.

10. Letter, 27 May 1923, quotation at Louis Baron and Pierre Leroy, *La Carrière Scientifique de Pierre Teilhard de Chardin* (Monaco: Editions du Rocher, 1964), 27.

11. Teilhard de Chardin, *The Human Phenomenon*, 187.

12. Ibid., 178.

13. Ibid., 67.

14. Ibid., 206.

15. Dominique Wang, *A Pékin avec Teilhard de Chardin* (Paris: Robert Laffont, 1981), 71–72.

BIBLIOGRAPHY

WORKS BY TEILHARD (IN FRENCH)

Teilhard de Chardin, Pierre. *Genèse d'une pensée: Lettres à Claude Aragonnès*. Paris: B. Grasset, 1961.

———. *Lettres inédites, 1923–1955: Lettres à l'abbé Gaudefroy et à l'abbé Breuil*. Monaco: Editions du Rocher, 1988.

———. *Oeuvres de Pierre Teilhard de Chardin*. Paris: Seuil, 1955–76.

Vol. 1, *Le phénomène humain*, 1955.

Vol. 2, *L'apparition de l'homme*, 1956.

Vol. 3, *La vision du passé*, 1957.

Vol. 4, *Le milieu divin*, 1957.

Vol. 5, *L'avenir de l'homme*, 1959.

Vol. 6, *L'énergie humaine*, 1962.

Vol. 7, *L'activation de l'énergie*, 1963.

Vol. 8, *La place de l'homme dans la nature*, 1956.

Vol. 9, *Science et Christ*, 1965.

Vol. 10, *Comment je crois*, 1969.

Vol. 11, *Les directions de l'avenir*, 1973.

Vol. 12, *Ecrits du temps de guerre*, 1976.

Vol. 13, *Le cœur de la matière*, 1976.

WORKS BY TEILHARD (IN ENGLISH)

Teilhard de Chardin, Pierre. *The Phenomenon of Man* (Le phénomène humain). Translated by Bernard Wall. London: Collins and New York: Harper and Row, 1959.

———. *The Human Phenomenon* (Le phénomène humain). Translated by Sarah Appleton-Weber. Brighton and Portland: Sussex Academic Press, 1999.

————. *The Divine Milieu* (Le milieu divin). Translator unidentified. London: Collins; New York: Harper and Row, 1960.

————. *Letters from a Traveler*. New York and Evanston: Harper and Row, 1962.

————. *The Future of Man* (L'avenir de l'homme). Translated by Norman Denny. London: Collins; New York: Harper and Row, 1964.

————. *Building the Earth* (Construire la terre). Translated by Noël Lindsay. Wilkes-Barre, Pa.: Dimension Books, 1965.

————. *Man's Place in Nature* (La place de l'homme dans la nature). Translated by René Hague. London: Collins; New York: Harper and Row, 1966.

————. *The Vision of the Past*. London: Collins; New York: Harper and Row, 1966.

————. *Science and Christ* (Science et Christ). Translated by René Hague. London: Collins; New York: Harcourt Brace Jovanovich, 1968.

————. *Writings in Time of War*. Translated by René Hague. New York and Evanston, Ill.: Harper and Row, 1968.

————. *Human Energy* (L'énergie humaine). Translated by J. M. Cohen. London: Collins; New York: Harcourt Brace Jovanovich, 1969.

————. *Activation of Energy* (L'activation de l'énergie). Translated by René Hague. London: Collins; New York: Harcourt Brace Jovanovich, 1970.

————. *Christianity and Evolution*. Translated by René Hague. New York: Harcourt Brace Jovanovich, 1971.

————. *The Heart of Matter* (Le cœur de la matière). Translated by René Hague. London: Collins; New York: Harcourt Brace Jovanovich, 1978.

WORKS ON TEILHARD

Baron, Louis, and Pierre Leroy. *La Carrière Scientifique de Pierre Teilhard de Chardin*. Monaco: Editions du Rocher, 1964.

Fabel, Arthur, and Donald St. John, eds. *Teilhard in the Twenty-First Century: The Emerging Spirit of the Earth.* Maryknoll, N.Y.: Orbis Books, 2003.

King, Ursula. *Spirit of Fire.* New York: Orbis Books Maryknoll, 1996.

———. *Towards a New Mysticism: Teilhard de Chardin and Eastern Religions.* London: Collins, 1980.

Lubac, Henri de. *La pensée religieuse du Père Pierre Teilhard de Chardin.* Paris: Aubier, 1962; Paris: Cerf, 2002.

Samson, Paul R., and David Pitt, eds. *The Biosphere and Noosphere Reader. Global Environment, Society and Change.* London and New York: Routledge, 1999.

Trennert-Hellwig, Mathias. *Die Urkraft des Kosmos: Dimensionen der Liebe im Werk Pierre Teilhards de Chardin.* Freiburg im Breisgau: Herder, 1993.

OTHER WORKS

Berry, Thomas. *The Great Work: Our Way into the Future.* New York: Bell Tower, 1999.

Csikszentmihalyi, Mihaly. *The Evolving Self: A Psychology for the Third Millenium.* New York: HarperCollins, 1993.

Muller, Robert. *New Genesis: Shaping Global Spirituality.* New York: Doubleday, 1982.

Pieper, Joseph. *Leisure, the Basis of Culture.* Translated by Gerald Malsbary. South Bend, Ind.: St. Augustine's Press. 1998.

Smith, Huston. *The Religions of Man.* New York: Harper, 1958.

Thurman, Howard. *Meditations of the Heart.* Boston: Beacon Press, 1981.

Science

Aspect, A., J. Dalibart, and R. Roger. *Physical Review Letters* 49 (1982): 1804.

Aspect, A., P. Grangier, and G. Roger. *Physical Review Letters* 47 (1981): 460.

Bell, J. S. 1965. "On the Einstein Podolsky Rosen Paradox." *Physics* 1 (1965): 195–200.

————. Interview. *Omni* 10, no. 8 (1988): 84–121.

Eddington, A. S. *The Nature of the Physical World.* New York: Macmillan, 1929.

————. *The Philosophy of Physical Science.* New York: Macmillan, 1939.

Eldredge, N. and S. J. Gould. In *Models of Paleobiology,* edited Thomas J. M. Schopf. San Francisco: Freeman, Cooper, 1972, 82–115.

d'Espagnat, B. *Physical Review Letters* 49 (1981): 1804.

Ewbank, J. D., L. Schäfer, and A. A. J. Ischenko, *Journal of Molecular Structure,* 321 (1994): 265–78.

Goswami, Amit, Richard E. Reed, and Maggie Goswami. *The Self-Aware Universe.* New York: Putnam, 1993.

Gould, J. S., and N. Eldredge. "Punctuated Equilibrium Comes of Age. *Nature* 366 (1993): 223–27.

Heisenberg, Werner. "Ideas of the Natural Philosophy of Ancient Times in Modern Physics." In *Philosophical Problems of Quantum Physics,* 1952; reprint, Woodbridge, Conn.: Ox Bow Press, 1979.

————. *Physics and Philosophy.* 1958; reprint, New York: Harper Torchbook, 1962.

Jeans, James. *The Mysterious Universe.* New York: Macmillan, 1931.

Jiang, X., M. Cao, B. Teppen, S. Q. Newton, and L. Schäfer. "Predictions of Protein Backbone Structural Parameters from First Principles: Systematic Comparisons of Calculated N-C(α)-C′, Angles with High-Resolution Protein Crystallographic Results." *Journal of Physical Chemistry* 99 (1995): 10521.

Kafatos, Menas, and Robert Nadeau. *The Conscious Universe: Parts and Whole in Physical Reality.* New York: Springer Verlag, 1990.

Margenau, Henry. *The Miracle of Existence.* Woodbridge, Conn.: Ox Bow Press, 1984.

Miller, Kenneth R. *Finding Darwin's God: A Scientist's Search for Common Ground between God and Evolution.* New York: Cliff Street Books, 1999.

Millett, F., and B. Durham. "Design of Photoactive Ruthenium Complexes to Study Interprotein Electron Transfer." *Biochemistry* 41 (2002): 11315–24.

Monod, Jacques. *Chance and Necessity.* London: Collins, 1972.

Nesteruk, A. V. "Is a Wave Function Collapse (WFC) a Real Event in Physical Space and Time?" In *Material Interpretations*, ed. M. C. Duffy and M. Wegener, vol. 2 of *Recent Advances in Relativity Theory*. Palm Harbor, Fla.: Hadronic Press, 2000, 169–70.

Polkinghorne, John. *Belief in God in an Age of Science*. New Haven: Yale University Press, 1998.

Ruse, Michael. *The Mysterious Universe*. New York: Macmillan, 1931.

———. "The Confessions of a Skeptic." *Research News and Opportunity in Science and Theology* 1, no. 6 (February 2001): 20.

———. "The Bad Smell of Anti-reductionism." *Research News and Opportunity in Science and Theology* 1, no. 9 (May 2001): 27.

Ruse, Michael, and E. O. Wilson. "The Approach of Sociobiology: The Evolution of Ethics." In *Religion and the Natural Sciences: The Range of Engagement*, edited by James E. Huchingson. Fort Worth, Texas: Harcourt, Brace, Jovanovich, 1993, 308–11.

Schäfer, Lothar. *In Search of Divine Reality*. University of Arkansas Press, 1997.

———. "On the Halfway Reductionism of Michael Ruse." *Research News and Opportunity in Science and Theology* 2, no. 4 (December 2001): 16.

———. "Quantum View of Evolution." *Research News and Opportunity in Science and Theology* 2, no. 8 (April 2002): 26.

———. "Biology Must Consider Quantum Effects." *Research News and Opportunity in Science and Theology* 3, no. 1 (September 2002): 16.

———. "Em Busca da Realidade Divina." Lisbon: Esquilo, 2003.

———. "Quantum Reality and the Importance of Consciousness in the Universe." In *Cons-Ciências, Centro Transcisciplinar de Estudos da Consciência*. Porto, Portugal: Universidade Fernando Pessoa, 2004, 81–102.

———. *Versteckte Wirklichkeit—Wie uns die Quantenphysik zur Transzendenz führt*. Stuttgart: Hirzel, 2004.

———. "Somos parte de un processo cosmico que esta em andamento." *IHU Online* 5 no. 140 (9 May 2005): 7–11.

Schäfer, Lothar, C. Van Alsenoy, and J. N. Scarsdale. "Ab Initio Studies of Structural Features not Easily Amenable to Experiment, 23. Molecular Structures and Conformational Analysis of the Dipeptide N-acetyl-N'-methyl Glycyl Amide and the Significance of Local Geometries for Peptide Structures. *Journal of Chemical Physics* 76 (1982): 1439.

Shimony, A. 1991. *Physics Today* 44 (August): 82–86.

Spetner, Lee M. *Not by Chance! Shattering the Modern Theory of Evolution.* New York: Judaica Press, 1997.

Srivastava, Jagdish. In *Thoughts on Synthesis of Science and Religion,* edited by T. D. Singh and S. Bandyopadhyay. Kolkata, India: Bhaktivedanta Institute, 2001, 157–74, 580–93.

———. "Scientific Exploration for a Spiritual Paradigm." *Savijnaanam: Journal of the Bhaktivedanta Institute* 1 (2002): 21–30.

Stapp, H. P. "Are Superluminal Connections Necessary?" *Nuovo Cimento* 40B (1977): 191–99.

Teppen, B. J., C.-H. Yu, S. Q. Newton, D. M. Miller, and L. Schäfer. "Quantum Molecular Dynamics Simulations Regarding the Dechlorination of Trichloro Ethene in the Interlayer Space of the 2:1 Clay Mineral Nontronite." *Journal of Physical Chemistry* 106 (2002): 5498–5503.

Van Alsenoy, C. , C.-H. Yu, A. Peeters, J. M. L. Martin, L. Schäfer. "Ab Initio Geometry Determination of Proteins. I. Crambin." *Journal of Physical Chemistry* (1998) 102: 2246–51.

Wheeler, John Archibald, and Kenneth Ford. *Geons, Black Holes, and Quantum Foam: A Life in Physics.* New York: Norton, 1998.

Wiener, Norbert. *Cybernetics.* 2d ed. New York: MIT Press, 1961.

Economy

de Foucauld, Jean-Baptiste. *Les Trois Cultures du Développement Humain.* Paris: Editions Odile Jacob, 2002.

John Paul II. *Laborem Exercens,* 1981.

John Paul II. *Centesimus Annus,* 1991.

Léon, Pierre. *L'ouverture du Monde XIVe–XVIe siècles.* Paris: Editions Armand Colin, 1977.

Landes, David S. *Richesse et Pauvreté des Nations.* Paris: Editions Albin Michel, 2000.

Maddison, Angus. *World Economy: A Millennial Perspective.* Paris: Development Centre of the Organisation for Economic Co-operation and Development, 2001.

China

Shiping Hua, *Scientism and Humanism: Two Cultures in Post-Mao China, 1978–1989*. Albany: State University of New York Press, 1995.

JEAN BOISSONNAT, a former member of the Council of Monetary Policy of the Bank of France, is the founder of the weekly magazine *Expansion* and the author of many books on economics, politics, and religion. He also contributes to the periodicals *Expansion, Ouest-France,* and *Journal du Dimanche.*

MICHEL CAMDESSUS is Honorary Governor of the Bank of France. He is French president Jacques Chirac's personal representative on Africa and also a member of the Commission for Africa, established by British prime minister Tony Blair in spring 2004. He has served as Governor of the Bank of France (November 1984–January 1987) and as Director General and Chairman of the Executive Board of the International Monetary Fund (January 1987–February 2000).

URSULA KING is professor emerita at the Department of Theology and Religious Studies, University of Bristol, England, and Professorial Research Associate, Centre for Gender and Religions Research, SOAS, University of London. She has published three books on Teilhard: *The Spirit of One Earth: Reflections on Teilhard de Chardin and Global Spirituality* (Orbis Books, 1997), *Christ in All Things: Exploring Spirituality with Teilhard de Chardin* (Orbis Books, 1997), and *Spirit of Fire: The Life and Vision of Teilhard de Chardin* (Orbis Books, 1998).

THOMAS M. KING, S.J., teaches at the Theology Department, Georgetown University, Washington, D.C. He is the author of *Teilhard and the Unity of Knowledge* (Paulist Press, 1983) and the editor, with Mary Wood Gilbert, of *Letters of Teilhard de Chardin and Lucile Swan* (Georgetown University Press, 1993).

HENRI MADELIN, S.J., is a professor at the Institut de Sciences Politiques (IEP) and at the Jesuit Faculties of Philosophy and Theology (Centre-Sèvres), both in Paris. He has served as provincial of the Jesuits in France. He is the author of many books in political philosophy and religion.

THIERRY MEYNARD, S.J., is professor of philosophy at Sun Yat-Sen University in Guangzhou, China. His articles and essays on Chinese philosophy and comparative philosophy and in the cross-cultural history of China and the West have been published in China, Taiwan, India, and the United States.

STEVEN C. ROCKEFELLER is professor emeritus and former Dean of Religion at Middlebury College, Vermont. He is the director of the Rockefeller Philanthropy Advisors and chair of Rockefeller Brothers Fund. He is the author *John Dewey, Religious Faith, and Democratic Humanism* (Columbia University Press, 1991, 1994). He is coeditor, with John C. Elder, of *Spirit and Nature: Why the Environment Is a Religious Issue: An Interfaith Dialogue* (Beacon Press, 1992), and, with Charles Taylor, Michael Waltzer, and Jurgen Habermas, of *Multiculturalism: Examining the Politics of Recognition* (Princeton University Press, 1994).

LOTHAR SCHÄFER is the E. Wertheim Distinguished Professor at the University of Arkansas Department of Chemistry and Biochemistry. He works in the domains of Physical Chemistry, Electron Diffraction, Applied Quantum Chemistry, and Computational Chemistry. He received the Fulbright College of Arts and Sciences Master Teacher Award in 1999. Since 1994, he has been serving on the editorial board of *Journal of Molecular Structure*. He has published more than 240 articles in refereed journals and some 25 book chapters and special essays. He has also published *In Search of Divine Reality—Science as a Source of Inspiration* (University of Arkansas Press, 1997), which has been translated into Russian and Portuguese.

MARY EVELYN TUCKER is a professor of religion at Bucknell University in Lewisburg, Pennsylvania, where she teaches courses in world religions, Asian religions, and religion and ecology. She is vice president of the American Teilhard Association, and codirector of the Forum on Religion and Ecology at Harvard University. She has published *Worldly Wonder: Religions Enter Their Ecological Phase* (Open Court Press, 2003) and *Moral and Spiritual Cultivation in Japanese Neo-Confucianism* (SUNY, 1989). She co-edited *Worldviews and Ecology* (Orbis Books, 1994) with John Grim, *Buddhism and Ecology* (Harvard/CSWR, 1997) with Duncan Williams, and *Confucianism and Ecology: The Interrelation of Heaven, Earth, and Humans* (CSWR, 1998) with John Berthrong.

Alexander, Samuel, 56
amorization, 29, 32, 74, 88
Anderson, J. G., 136
Annan, Kofi, 84
Augustine of Hippo, Saint, 110

Bell, John, 111
Bergson, Henri, 56
Berry, Thomas, 17, 44
biosphere, 7–10, 15, 35, 55, 57, 114,
    122, 124, 151
Black, Davidson, 136
Blair, Tony, 84
Boule, Marcellin, 148
Bruno, Giordano, 95

chastity, ix, 32–33
Chaunu, Pierre, 92
Chen, Duxiu, 138
Christ, x, 23, 26, 29, 33, 36, 39, 73–
    74, 89, 103, 134
Christianity, x, 24, 74, 95, 102–6
Christogenesis, 103
community, 50, 51, 54, 59, 61–64,
    81, 85, 105, 153
  Earth, 44, 52, 53, 55, 58, 64
  faith communities, 66
  global, ix, 3, 6, 15, 59–60, 66–67,
    71–73, 80
  human, 4–5, 13–14, 16, 18, 104
  international, 85, 87
  Jesuit, 20

complexity, 43, 45, 51, 61–62, 80,
    118–19, 149, 154
consciousness, x, 6, 8, 15–16, 39, 44,
    46, 50, 51, 53, 57, 64, 66–67,
    89–90, 102, 109–12, 118, 126–
    34, 147, 149–55
  cosmic, 111
  global, 104
  greater, 10, 37
  spiritual, 59, 60
  superconsciousness, 153
  of elementary particles, 133
convergence, 11, 37, 61, 74, 80–81,
    84, 90, 102, 130, 149, 153
cosmogenesis, 45, 50–51, 62, 64
cosmology, ix, 44, 48, 50
creativity, ix, 45, 54, 79
Csikszentmihalyi, Mihaly, 53

Darwin, Charles, 113, 122, 125–26,
    145–46, 150
Dawkins, Richard, 125
Deng, Xiaoping, 142
Descartes, René, 93
Dewey, John, 56, 138
Diderot, Denis, 26
Ding, Wenjiang, 138–41, 143
divinization, 36, 72–74
Domenach, Jean-Luc, 75
Dupuy, Jean-Pierre, 92

Earth, ix, 4, 7, 8–10, 17, 19, 22, 26,
    32, 34–35, 44–45, 47, 49–52
  future of, 149

sense of the, 7, 10, 11
soul of the, 31
thinking, 15, 55, 57
See also community, Earth; spirit,
Earth
Earth Charter, ix, 9, 57–67
ecology, viii, 44, 87, 99
economy, ix, 67, 76–77, 79, 91–93,
97–98, 139, 142
Eddington, A. S., 112–13
energy, 6, 7, 11, 14, 19, 30, 46, 49,
55, 64, 110, 111, 113, 115–17,
143, 151–52
human, 14,16
spiritual, viii, 3, 4, 13–15, 17–
18, 55, 152
environment, vii, 7, 9, 16, 19, 24, 60,
61, 63, 79, 83, 99, 145
environmentalists, x, 24, 43
evolution, x, 6–7, 9–10, 16, 21, 30,
35, 38–39, 44, 45, 47–55, 57–59,
64, 127–31, 139, 145–47, 149–
51, 153–55
biological, *x*, 5, 57, 109, 114, 120,
123, 128, 145
spiritual, 11, 13
evolutionary process, 9, 49, 51–52,
54, 57–58, 61, 151

faith, 4, 5, 13, 15–16, 35, 39, 53, 60,
104, 148–49, 154–55
Christian, 95, 154
personal, vii
See also World Congress of Faith
in humanity, 16, 154
in science, 138
feminine, the, ix, 32–33
Foucauld, Jean-Baptiste de, 75
Futumya, Douglas, 113

Galileo Galilei, 93, 95
Gaudefroy, Christophe, 80
global communities. See *community,
global*
global ethics, 18, 56–60, 67

globalization, viii– ix, 29, 31, 57, 60,
64, 71, 75–83, 89–106
God, viii, 11, 16, 22–28, 35, 39, 57–
58, 73–75, 88–91, 95, 103–4,
106, 113, 130, 147, 154
personal, viii, 23, 26–28
Gorbachev, Mikhail, 60
Gould, Stephen, 148
Grabau, Amadeus, 136

Havel, Václav, 87
hominization, 55, 151
Hu, Shi, 138, 140–42
Hua, Shiping, 142
humanity, ix, 3, 5, 7,–8, 10–11, 13,
16, 21–22, 26–27, 30, 34–36,
54, 57–59, 62, 64, 66, 73–74, 80,
90–95, 98–99, 102–4, 106, 126,
141, 149, 151, 154
failed, viii, 34
future of, viii–x, 4–6, 17, 19, 22–
23, 29, 71, 74–75, 81
growth of, 3, 33, 146
impersonal, 27
new, 35
superior, 140
See also faith, in humanity

Jeans, James, 112
John XXIII, 82
John of the Cross, Saint, 87
John Paul II, 78, 84, 95

Kepler, Johannes, 93
Kropotkin, Pyotr, 146

Landes, David, 95
Le Roy, Edouard, 8
Leibniz, Gottfried Wilhelm, 93
Levitt, Theodore, 89
Li, Dazhao, 138
Liang, Shuming, 143–47, 152–55
Licent, Emile, 136
Louis XIV, 105
Lovelock, James, 10
Lubac, Henri de, 39, 87

Maddison, Angus, 94
Margeneau, Henry, 112
matter, *ix–x*, 8, 14, 29–30, 32, 39, 45, 49–50, 55, 90, 110, 112–18, 125–28, 130, 139, 144, 147, 151–52
Miller, Kenneth, 113
Montesquieu, 101
Mounier, Emmanuel, 73
Muller, Robert, 18

Newton, Isaac, 93, 126
noosphere, 3, 7–11, 13–16, 29, 31–33, 57–58, 86–87, 128, 154

O'Connell, Robert, S.J., xi
Ockham, William of, 119
omega, x, 24, 29, 36, 74, 91, 129–30, 150–51, 154

Paul, Saint, 23–24, 74
Perroux, François, 73
personalization, viii, 5, 29, 30, 34, 80–81, 84, 130
Pieper, Joseph, 27
Pitt, David, 9
planetization, ix, 55, 57, 80
Plato, 57, 110, 118
Plotinus, 51
progress, 12–13, 35, 44, 67, 77–80, 82–83, 87, 100–1, 139, 149–51, 153

Raiser, Konrad, 104
Rilke, Rainer Maria, 88
Ruse, Michael, 125

Samson, Paul, 9
Schrödinger, Erwin, 110
science, viii, *x*, 6, 8, 17, 21, 35, 37, 44, 56, 59, 61, 66–67, 75, 95, 109, 113, 125, 127–28, 130–32, 134–55
  facts of, viii, 144
  natural, 141, 145, 147

modern, 15, 136, 140, 151
  social, 138, 141, 147
Sesé, Bernard, 91
Smith, Huston, 131
spirit, 8, 11–13, 16, 18, 29–30, 32, 38–39, 50, 73, 84, 86–87, 90, 139, 151, 153–54
  human, viii, 36, 52–53, 88, 138–39, 143, 151
  of the Earth, 10, 49, 56–57
spiritual energy. *See* energy, spiritual
spirituality, 10, 16–18
  new, 16
  human, 88
Stapp, H. P., 112
Strong, Maurice, 60
Suess, Eduard, 7–8
sustainable development, 60–61, 64–66, 86, 99
Thant, U, 18
Thurman, Howard, 6
Trennert-Hellwig, M., 127
UNESCO, 5, 66
United Nations, viii, 5, 9, 18, 60–61, 63, 65–67, 71, 82, 85, 99
unity, 4, 8, 10, 104, 139, 141, 145, 149, 151, 153, 155
  human, 5, 11, 13, 64
  of human family, vii
  organic, 8, 31

Wheeler, John Archibald, 111, 117
Whitehead, Alfred North, 56
Wiener, Norbert, 112
Williams, Day, 56
Wilson, E. O., 125
within, viii–x, 45, 49–50, 132
World Congress of Faith, 4, 6, 15

Younghusband, Francis, 4

zest for life, viii–ix, 3, 6–7, 9, 11, 13–17, 19, 43, 45, 47, 49, 51–53, 55
Zhang, Junmai, 137–40, 142–43
Zola, Emile, 25